HAMLYN POCKET GUIDES

GERMAN

PHRASE BOOK AND DICTIONARY

HAMLYN POCKET GUIDES

GERMAN

PHRASE BOOK AND DICTIONARY

compiled by

LEXUS

with Petra Firsching

HAMLYN

First published 1989 by
The Hamlyn Publishing Group Limited
Michelin House, 81 Fulham Road
LONDON SW3 6RB

ISBN 0 600 56432 0

Printed in Great Britain

INTRODUCTION

This new phrase book and dictionary has been designed to combine a large number of features in a single integrated package.

A total of 101 concise sections, arranged in alphabetical order, give you information on how to deal with a variety of situations in German. Flicking through the book and looking at the headings at the tops of the pages will give you an instant guide to the contents list.

There are sections for activities such as shopping, driving, changing money, buying a ticket, ordering a meal etc.

There are sections which enable you to express reactions, to express your feelings, likes, dislikes, emotions etc. Sections for making requests, for talking about yourself and for understanding people.

And the nuts and bolts of the language are clearly presented in straightforward grammar sections so that you can go further with your German and develop some skill in the language.

And for deciphering German signs a comprehensive list of things you're likely to see when travelling abroad has been included – in addition to a menu reader and drinks list. And as well as this a number of typical responses that you might get from German people if you say something or ask a question in German have been included.

All the phrases are provided with an easy-to-use pronunciation guide (see below) and there are also guidelines on the pronunciation of German.

And so that you can build up your German vocabulary and make modifications to the phrases given in the various sections, this book also includes a 3,000 word dictionary of English into German.

Some notes on the pronunciation system used

The pronunciation guide in this book is based on writing out German words as though they were English words. So if you read out the pronunciation line as English you will communicate with a German person. (For more information on German pronunciation, see *PRONUNCIATION*). Some special conventions have been used.

ew	put your mouth to say oo then say ee
ī	like the i sound in 'tie' or 'cry'
j	like the s sound in 'measure' or the z sound in 'seizure'
K	like the ch sound in the Scottish pronunciation of 'loch'
oo	as in 'took' or 'crook'
OO	as in 'moon' or 'croon'
ow	as in 'down' or 'town'

Letters in bold print in the pronunciation guide show which part of a word is to be stressed.

Translations of 'you'

In most cases 'you' has been translated with the polite form **Sie**. Where two translations are given for 'you' the first is the polite **Sie** form and the second the familiar **du** form. For more on this see PRONOUNS.

ACCEPTING, SAYING YES

Yes please.
Ja, bitte.
ya bittuh

Thank you.
Vielen Dank.
feelen dank

Yes, I'd like to.
Ja, gerne.
ya gairnuh

Yes, that would be very nice.
Ja, das wäre sehr nett.
ya dass vairuh zair net

Ok, fine.
Ja, in Ordnung.
ya in ortnoong

Yes, I'd love one.
Ja, gerne.
ya gairnuh

I'll take two.
Ich hätte gerne zwei.
ish hettuh gairnuh tsvī

That's just right thanks.
Prima, vielen Dank.
preema feelen dank

Great, good idea!
Prima, gute Idee!
preema gOOtuh eeday

ADJECTIVES

When an adjective is not placed directly in front of a noun then you just use the form of the adjective as given in the dictionary in this book, for example:

It's COLD.
Es ist KALT.
ess ist kalt

Is this ticket VALID?
ist diese Fahrkarte GÜLTIG?
ist deezuh farkartuh gewltik

If an adjective is used in front of a noun then it has to agree with the noun – that is to say, it needs an ending:

A COLD day.
Ein KALTER Tag.
īn kalter tahk

A VALID ticket.
Eine GÜLTIGE Fahrkarte.
īnuh gewltiguh farkartuh

There are two main sets of endings for adjectives. One set is used after the words for 'a' – **ein** or **eine**. The second set is used after the words for 'the' – **der** (masculine), **die** (feminine), **das** (neuter). In each set the endings differ according to both the case (*see CASES*) and the gender of the noun.

endings after **ein(e)**

	singular *masc*	*fem*	*neuter*	*plural* *all genders*
nom	**-er**	**-e**	**-es**	**-e**
acc	**-en**	**-e**	**-es**	**-e**
gen	**-en**	**-en**	**-en**	**-er**
dat	**-en**	**-en**	**-en**	**-en**

endings after **der, die, das**

	singular *masc*	*fem*	*neuter*	*plural* *all genders*
nom	**-e**	**-e**	**-e**	**-en**
acc	**-en**	**-e**	**-e**	**-en**
gen	**-en**	**-en**	**-en**	**-en**
dat	**-en**	**-en**	**-en**	**-en**

Examples:

A yellow car.
Ein gelbes Auto.
īn gelbess owto

The yellow car.
Das gelbe Auto.
dass gelbuh owto

The driver of the yellow car.
Der Fahrer des gelben Autos.
dair farer dess gelben owtos

She drove off in a yellow car.
Sie fuhr in einem gelben Auto davon.
zee fOOr in īnem gelben owto dafon

AGREEING WITH PEOPLE

That's right.
Das stimmt.
dass shtimmt

No, you're quite right.
Nein, Sie haben ganz recht.
nīn zee hahben gants resht

Oh yes.
Oh ja.
o ya

That's just what I think.
Ich bin ganz Ihrer Meinung.
ish bin gants eerer mīnoong

Absolutely.
Ganz genau.
gants genow

You were right.
Sie hatten ganz recht.
zee hatten gants resht

He agrees with me.
Er ist meiner Meinung.
air ist mīner mīnoong

So do/am I.
Ich auch.
ish owK

Nor do/am I.
Ich auch nicht.
ish owK nisht

ALPHABET

(*see also PRONUNCIATION*)

The alphabet in German is pronounced as follows:

a *ah*
b *bay*
c *tsay*
d *day*
e *ay*
f *ef*
g *gay*
h *hah*
i *ee*
j *yot*
k *kah*
l *el*
m *em*
n *en*
o *oh*
p *pay*
q *koo*
r *air*
s *ess*
t *tay*
u *oo*
v *fow*
w *vay*
x *iks*
y *ewpseelon*
z *tset*

To spell your name, Harris, in German you would say:
hah-ah-air-air-ee-ess

In German there is also another letter written **ß**. This is called an **Eszett** (*ess-tset*) and is equivalent to a double s.

ANNOYANCE

Bother! Damn!
Mist! Verdammt!
mist fairdammt

It's very annoying.
Das ist sehr ärgerlich.
dass ist zair airgerlish

That's totally impossible.
Das ist völlig unmöglich.
dass ist furlik oonmurglish

Don't be silly.
Seien Sie/sei nicht albern.
zīen zee/zī nisht albern

Rubbish!
Unsinn!
oonzin

Of course not!
Natürlich nicht!
natewrlish nisht

What do you expect!
Was erwarten Sie denn!
vass airvarten zee denn

Oh, come on now!
Nun seien Sie/sei mal vernünftig!
nOOn zīen zee/zī mal fairnewnftik

You idiot!
Sie/du Idiot!
zee/dOO id-yoht

APOLOGIES

Sorry!
Entschuldigung!
entshooldigoong

Pardon?
Wie bitte?
vee bittuh

I'm very sorry.
Es tut mir sehr leid.
ess tOOt meer zair līt

RESPONSES

Das ist schon in Ordnung.
dass ist shohn in ortnoong
That's ok.

Das macht nichts.
dass mahKt nishts
It doesn't matter.

He says he's very sorry.
Es tut ihm sehr leid.
ess tOOt eem zair līt

Please accept my apologies.
Ich bitte vielmals um Entschuldigung.
ish bittuh feelmalss oom entshooldigoong

I feel awful.
Das ist mir sehr unangenehm.
dass ist meer zair oonan-genaym

How much did it cost?
Wieviel hat es gekostet?
veefeel hat ess gekostet

ARTICLES

There are three genders in German: masculine (*m*), feminine (*f*) and neuter (*n*). Each has its own article.

The definite article (the) for masculine nouns is **der** *dair* and the indefinite article (a, an) is **ein** *īn*:

der/ein Mann	the/a man

For feminine nouns the word for 'the' is **die** *dee* and the word for 'a' is **eine** *īnuh*:

die/eine Bar	the/a bar

For neuter nouns the word for 'the' is **das** *dass* and the word for 'a' is **ein** *īn*:

das/ein Mädchen	the/a girl

In the plural all three genders have the same definite article – **die** *dee*:

die Männer	the men
die Bars	the bars
die Mädchen	the girls

The form of each article varies according to the case that is being used. The four cases are: nominative, accusative, genitive or dative. Plurals also have the same four cases. The definite article (the) has the following forms. (*see also CASES*):

	m	*f*	*n*	*pl*
nom	**der**	**die**	**das**	**die**
acc	**den**	**die**	**das**	**die**
gen	**des**	**der**	**der**	**die**
dat	**dem**	**der**	**dem**	**den**

The indefinite article (a, an) has these forms:

nom	**ein**	**eine**	**ein**
acc	**einen**	**eine**	**ein**
gen	**eines**	**einer**	**eines**
dat	**einem**	**einer**	**einem**

ATTENTION: GETTING PEOPLE'S ATTENTION

Excuse me!
Entschuldigen Sie bitte!
*entshooldigen zee **bi**ttuh*

Hello!
Hallo!
***ha**llo*

Waiter!
Herr Ober!
*hair **oh**ber*

Waitress!
Fräulein!
***froy**līn*

Miss!
Fräulein!
***froy**līn*

Mr Schmidt!
Herr Schmidt!
hair shmit

Mrs Müller!
Frau Müller!
*frow **mew**ller*

Is there anyone there?
Ist da jemand?
*ist da **yay**mant*

Hoy you!
He Sie!
hay zee

BANKS

Could I change this into German marks?
Könnte ich dies in D-Mark umtauschen?
kurntuh ish deess in daymark oomtowshen

I want to draw cash on this credit card.
Ich möchte gerne mit dieser Kreditkarte Bargeld abheben.
ish murshtuh gairnuh mit deezer kredeetkartuh bargelt aphayben

I'd like to cash these traveller's cheques.
Ich möchte gerne diese Reiseschecks einlösen.
ish murshtuh gairnuh deezuh rīzuh-shecks īnlurzen

Can I cash this cheque here?
Kann ich diesen Scheck hier einlösen?
kan ish deezen sheck heer īnlurzen

This is the phone number of my bank at home.
Dies ist die Telefonnummer meiner eigenen Bank.
deess ist dee telefohn-noommer mīner īgenen bank

RESPONSES

Könnte ich bitte Ihren Paß sehen?
kurntuh ish bittuh eeren pas zayen
Could I see your passport?

Sie bekommen Ihr Geld an der Kasse.
zee bekommen eer gelt an dair kassuh
You get your money at the cash desk.

Could you give me some small change as well?
Könnte ich bitte auch etwas Kleingeld bekommen?
kurntuh ish bittuh owK etvass klīn-gelt bekommen

Can you change this into smaller notes?
Können Sie dies in kleine Scheine umtauschen?
kurnen zee deess in klīnuh shīnuh oomtowshen

BEACH, THE POOL

Let's go down to the beach.
Laß uns zum Strand gehen.
lass oonss tsoom shtrant gayen

I'm going to the pool.
Ich gehe ins Schwimmbad.
ish gayuh inss shvimbaht

They're on the beach.
Sie sind am Strand.
zee zint am shtrant

Can we have one of those beach chair things?
Können wir einen von diesen Strandkörben bekommen?
kurnen veer īnen fon deezen shtrant-kurben bekommen

Where do you get the towels from?
Wo bekommt man Handtücher?
vo bekommt man hant-tewsher

Can I have a recliner?
Könnte ich einen Liegestuhl bekommen?
kurntuh ish īnen leeguh-shtOOl bekommen

Are you coming in?
Kommen Sie/kommst du ins Wasser?
kommen zee/komst dOO inss vasser

I can't swim.
Ich kann nicht schwimmen.
ish kan nisht shvimmen

Baden verboten.
bahden fairbohten
No bathing.

BUSES AND TRAMS

Which bus goes to . . .?
Welcher Bus fährt nach . . .?
velsher booss fayrt nahK

Does this tram go to . . .?
Fährt diese Bahn nach . . .?
fayrt deezuh bahn nahK

When's the next bus to . . .?
Wann fährt der nächste Bus nach . . .?
van fayrt dair nexstuh booss nahK

Is there a bus that goes there?
Gibt es dorthin eine Busverbindung?
geept ess dorthin īnuh boossfairbindoong

What time does the bus go back?
Um wieviel Uhr fährt der Bus zurück?
oom veefeel OOr fayrt dair booss tsOOrewk

When does the last tram leave?
Wann fährt die letzte Straßenbahn?
van fayrt dee lets-tuh shtrahssenbahn

A single to . . .
Eine einfache Fahrkarte nach . . .
īnuh īnfahKuh farkartuh nahK

Two returns to . . .
Zwei Rückfahrkarten nach . . .
tsvī rewkfarkarten nahK

Could you tell me when to get off?
Sagen Sie mir Bescheid, wenn ich aussteigen muß?
zahgen zee meer beshīt ven ish owss-shtīgen mooss

Haltestelle.
haltuh-shtelluh
Bus/tram stop.

BUSINESS TRAVEL

I'm here on business.
Ich bin geschäftlich hier.
ish bin gesheftlish heer

James O'Connor to see Mr ...
James O'Connor, ich habe einen Termin mit Herrn ...
James O'Connor ish hahbuh īnen tairmeen mit hairn

My company is ...
Meine Firma heißt ...
mīnuh feerma hīst

I'll wait.
Ich warte.
ish vartuh

Do you have a card?
Haben Sie eine Karte?
hahben zee īnuh kartuh

We'd like to get this firmed up.
Wir möchten das gerne unter Dach und Fach bringen.
veer murshten dass gairnuh oonter dahK oont fahK bring-en

Can you give us more time?
Können Sie uns noch etwas Zeit geben?
kurnen zee oonss noK etvass tsīt gayben

I'll get them faxed over.
Ich schicke sie per Telefax.
ish shickuh zee pair telefax

It's a pleasure doing business with you.
Es ist ein Vergnügen, mit Ihnen Geschäfte zu machen.
ess ist īn fairg-newgen mit eenen gesheftuh tsOO mahKen

Auf gute Zusammenarbeit.
owf gOOtuh tsOOzammenarbīt
Here's to a good working relationship.

CAMPING

Excuse me, do you know where the nearest campsite is?
Entschuldigung, wissen Sie, wo der nächste Campingplatz ist?
entshooldigoong vissen zee vo dair nexstuh kemping-plats ist

Can we camp here?
Können wir hier zelten?
kurnen veer heer tselten

Can you give us a camping pass?
Können Sie uns einen Campingpaß ausstellen?
kurrnen zee oonss īnen kemping-pas owss-shtellen

How much is it per night?
Wieviel kostet es pro Nacht?
veefeel kostet ess pro nahkt

We'd like to stay one night/two nights.
Wir möchten gerne eine Nacht/zwei Nächte bleiben.
veer murshten gairnuh īnuh nahkt/tsvī neshtuh blīben

Is this drinking water?
Ist dies hier Trinkwasser?
ist deess heer trinkvasser

Do you sell calor gas?
Verkaufen Sie Butangas?
fairkowfen zee bootahn-gahss

Which way to the shops?
Wo sind hier die Geschäfte?
vo zint heer dee gesheftuh

Do you have a map with campsites on it?
Haben Sie eine Karte, auf der Campingplätze eingetragen sind?
hahben zee īnuh kartuh owf dair kemping-pletsuh īn-getrahgen zint

CAR ACCIDENTS

He came straight out.
Er fuhr einfach heraus.
air foor īnfahK hairowss

He didn't look.
Er hat nicht aufgepaßt.
air hat nisht owf-gepast

She was going far too fast.
Sie ist viel zu schnell gefahren.
zee ist feel tsoo shnel gefaren

He went through the red light.
Er hat die Ampel bei Rot überfahren.
air hat dee ampel bī roht ewberfaren

She reversed into me.
Sie hat mich rückwärts angefahren.
zee hat mish rewkvairts an-gefaren

She didn't indicate.
Sie hat nicht geblinkt.
zee hat nisht geblinkt

He was on the wrong side of the road.
Er fuhr auf der falschen Straßenseite.
air foor owf dair falshen shtrahssen-zītuh

Ok, it was my fault.
Ja gut, es war meine Schuld.
ya goot ess var mīnuh shoolt

Did you see that?
Haben Sie das gesehen?
hahben zee dass gezayen

Will you be a witness for me?
Würden Sie als Zeuge/Zeugin für mich aussagen?
vewrden zee alss tsoyguh/tsoygin fewr mish owss-zahgen

Can you write down your name and address?
Können Sie Ihren Namen und Adresse aufschreiben?
kurnen zee eeren nahmen oont adressuh owf-shrīben

Do you want to settle this between ourselves?
Wollen wir das zwischen uns ausmachen?
vollen veer das tsvishen oonss owss-mahKen

Could you call the police?
Könnten Sie die Polizei rufen?
kurnten zee dee politsī rOOfen

I'm ok, I'm not hurt.
Ich bin okay, ich bin unverletzt.
ish bin okay ish bin oonfairletst

She's been injured.
Sie ist verletzt.
zee ist fairletst

Learn to drive!
Lernen Sie erst mal Autofahren!
lairnen zee airst mal owto-faren

CASES

(*see also* *ARTICLES, PRONOUNS*)

German has four cases. They are called: nominative, accusative, genitive and dative.
The ***NOMINATIVE*** is used for words which are the subject of a sentence:

Der Computer (*nom*) **ist nicht so teuer.**
dair kompyooter ist nisht zo toyer
The computer isn't so expensive.

The ***ACCUSATIVE*** is used for words which are the object of a sentence:

Er hat einen Computer (*acc*) **gekauft.**
air hat īnen kompyooter gekowft
He has bought a computer.

The accusative is also used after certain prepositions (as indicated in the dictionary section):

Ohne einen Mantel.
ohnuh īnen mantel
Without a coat.

Für Ihren Mann.
fewr eeren man
For your husband.

The ***GENITIVE*** is used to indicate possession:

Der Preis des Computers.
dair prīss dess kompyooters
The price of the computer.

Note that an **s** is added to masculine and neuter nouns when used in the genitive.

The ***DATIVE*** is used to indicate motion towards something or someone:

Er hat den Computer (*acc*) **seinem Bruder** (*dat*) **geschenkt.**
air hat dayn kompyooter zīnem brOOder geshenkt
He gave the computer to his brother.

The dative is also used after certain prepositions (as indicated in the dictionary section):

Mit dem Computer.	**Hinter den Büchern**
mit daym kompyooter	*hinter dayn bewshern*
With the computer.	Behind the books.

As shown in the dictionary section, some prepositions can take either the accusative or the dative. These are:

an	on, to
auf	on
hinter	behind
in	in
neben	beside
über	over
unter	under
vor	in front of
zwischen	between

Where the idea of motion is involved then the accusative case is used:

It fell to the floor.
Es fiel auf den Fußboden.
ess feel owf dayn fooss-bohden

I got on the tram.
Ich stieg in die Bahn ein.
ish shteek in dee bahn īn

The dative, on the other hand, is used to express position:

It's on the floor.
Es ist auf dem Fußboden.
ess ist owf daym fooss-bohden

I was sitting on the tram.
Ich saß in der Bahn.
ish sahss in dair bahn

CHEMIST

Is there a chemist open today?
Hat hier heute eine Apotheke geöffnet?
hat heer ***hoy****tuh īnuh apo****tay****kuh ge-****ur****fnet*

Is there a chemist open at nights?
Hat eine Apotheke nachts geöffnet?
*hat īnuh apo****tay****kuh nahKts ge-****ur****fnet*

Have you got something for . . . ?
Haben Sie etwas gegen . . . ?
hah*ben zee etvass* ***gay****gen*

Do you have something equivalent to this?
Haben Sie etwas ähnliches wie dieses?
hah*ben zee etvass* ***ay****nlishess vee deezes*

Can you make up this prescription?
Können Sie dieses Rezept zubereiten?
kur*nen zee deezess retsept tsOOberīten*

YOU'LL SEE

Nur zur äußerlichen Anwendung.
nOOr tsOOr ***oy****sserlishen* ***an****vendoong*
Not to be taken internally.

Vor dem Essen einzunehmen.
for daym essen ***īn****tsOOnaymen*
Take before meals.

Vor Kindern schützen.
for ***kin****dern shewtsen*
Keep out of reach of children.

Vor Gebrauch schütteln.
*for gebr****owK*** *shewteln*
Shake before use.

CHILDREN AND BABIES

Is there a crèche?
Gibt es hier eine Kinderkrippe?
geept ess heer īnuh kinderkrippuh

We need a baby-sitter for tonight.
Wir brauchen für heute abend einen Babysitter.
veer browKen fewr hoytuh ahbent īnen 'babysitter'

We'll be back at . . .
Wir kommen um . . . Uhr zurück.
veer kommen oom . . . OOr tsOOrewk

Can we have a children's portion please?
Können wir bitte eine Kinderportion bekommen?
kurnen veer bittuh īnuh kinder-ports-yohn bekommen

Two adults and one child to . . .
Zwei Erwachsene und ein Kind nach . . .
tsvī airvakzenuh oont īn kint nahK

RESPONSES

Wie alt ist er/sie?
vee alt ist air/zee
How old is he/she?

He/she is . . . years/months old.
Er/sie ist . . . Jahre/Monate alt.
air/zee ist . . . yahruh/mohnahtuh alt

Isn't he/she lovely!
Ist er/sie nicht süß!
ist air/zee nisht zewss

CINEMA AND THEATRE

Do you have a programme of what's on in Berlin?
Haben Sie ein Veranstaltungsprogramm von Berlin?
hahben zee īn fair-anshtaltoongs-program fon bairleen

I'd like to go to the cinema/theatre.
Ich möchte gerne ins Kino/Theater gehen.
ish murshtuh gairnuh inss keeno/tayahter gayen

I want to see a German film/play.
Ich möchte einen deutschen Film/ein deutsches Theaterstück sehen.
ish murshtuh īnen doytshen film/īn doytshess tayahterstewk zayen

Can I book two seats for this evening?
Kann ich für heute abend zwei Karten buchen?
kan ish fewr hoyh ahbent tsvī karten bOOKen

In the stalls/in the balcony.
Im Parkett/auf dem Rang.
im parket/owf daym rang

How much are tickets for the stalls/for the balcony?
Wieviel kosten die Karten für das Parkett/den Rang?
veefeel kosten dee karten fewr dass parket/dayn rang

I'll pick them up later on.
Ich hole sie später ab.
ish hohluh zee shpayter ap

I'll meet you in the foyer.
Wir treffen uns im Foyer.
veer treffen oons im fwī-ay

Is there a concession for students/children?
Gibt es Ermäßigungen für Studenten/Kinder?
geept ess airmaysigoong-en fewr shtOOdenten/kinder

CLEANING THINGS

Where's the nearest dry cleaner's/launderette?
Wo ist die nächste Reinigung/der nächste Waschsalon?
voh ist dee nexstuh rīnigoong/dair nexstuh vash-zalon

Can you clean this coat for me?
Können Sie diesen Mantel für mich reinigen?
kurnen zee deezen mantel fewr mish rīnigen

When will they be ready?
Wann sind sie fertig?
van zint zee fairtik

RESPONSES

Heute nachmittag.
hoytuh nahKmitahk
This afternoon.

Morgen.
morgen
Tomorrow.

Übermorgen.
ewbermorgen
The day after tomorrow.

Do you have some clothes pegs?
Haben Sie ein paar Wäscheklammern?
hahben zee īn par veshuh-klammern

Is it ok if I hang my washing out here?
Kann ich meine Wäsche hier aufhängen?
kan ish mīnuh veshuh heer owfheng-en

COMMANDS

One way to express commands in German is to take the form of the verb as given in the dictionary section in this book and then add the word **Sie** *zee* after it. For example, the verb 'to wait' is **warten**. The command (or imperative) 'wait!' is **warten Sie!**

If you are talking to someone with whom you are using the **du** form of the verb (*see PRONOUNS*), then the imperative is expressed by removing the final **n** from the form as given in the dictionary part of this book. For example, 'wait!' is **warte!**

But if you are using this form, then you should also check the second column of the list of irregular verbs in the section on the ***PAST TENSE***. For example 'read it' would be either:

lesen Sie es!
layzen zee ess

or **lies es!**
leess ess

Some examples:

Come here!
Kommen Sie/komm her!
kommen zee/kom hair

Don't wait for me.
Warten Sie/warte nicht auf mich.
varten zee/vartuh nisht owf mish

Don't speak so fast.
Sprechen Sie/sprich nicht so schnell.
shpreshen zee/sprish nisht zo shnel

Stop that!
Hören Sie/hör auf!
huren zee/hur owf

COMPARISONS

To say that something is, for example, MORE beautiful or that something is fastER than something else you use a comparative form of the adjective (or adverb). In German these are all formed by adding the ending **-er** to the adjective:

fast	**schnell**	*shnel*
faster	**schneller**	*shneller*
beautiful	**schön**	*shurn*
more beautiful	**schöner**	*shurner*

Are there any cheaper seats?
Gibt es billigere Plätze?
geept ess billigeruh pletsuh

Do you have any bigger ones?
Haben Sie größere?
hahben zee grursseruh

Could you speak a bit more slowly please?
Könnten Sie bitte etwas langsamer sprechen?
kurnten zee bittuh etvass langzahmer shpreshen

To say that something is, for example, the MOST beautiful or the fastEST, you use the superlative form of the adjective (or adverb). This is formed by adding **-ste** to the adjective:

fast	**schnell**	*shnel*
fastest	**schnellste**	*shnelstuh*
beautiful	**schön**	*shurn*
most beautiful	**schönste**	*shurnstuh*

Which is the quietest room?
Welches ist das ruhigste Zimmer?
velshess ist das rOO-igstuh tsimmer

Some forms are irregular:

gut	*goot*	good
besser	*besser*	better
beste	*bestuh*	best
hoch	*hohK*	high
höher	*hur-er*	higher
höchste	*hurK-stuh*	highest

Some more examples:

This one is better THAN that one.
Dies hier ist besser ALS das da.
deess heer ist besser alss dass da

It wasn't AS hard AS I thought.
Es war nicht SO schwer WIE ich dachte.
ess var nisht zo shvair vee ish daKtuh

AS fast AS possible.
SO schnell WIE möglich.
zo shnel vee murglish

COMPLAINTS

The . . . isn't working.
Der/die/das . . . funktioniert nicht.
dair/dee/dass . . . foonkt-syohneert nisht

There's no light in my room.
In meinem Zimmer ist kein Licht.
in mīnem tsimmer ist kīn lisht

There's no toilet paper.
Es ist kein Toilettenpapier da.
ess ist kīn twaletten-papeer da

There's something wrong with this.
Hiermit stimmt etwas nicht.
heermit shtimmt etvass nisht

It tastes very peculiar.
Das schmeckt ganz merkwürdig.
dass shmeckt gants mairkvewrdik

It's still not right.
Es ist immer noch nicht in Ordnung.
ess ist immer noK nisht in ortnoong

I'm not happy about it.
Ich bin damit nicht zufrieden.
ish bin damit nisht tsOOfreeden

I want my money back.
Ich möchte mein Geld zurückhaben.
ish murshtuh mīn gelt tsOOrewk-hahben

I really think you should accept responsibility.
Ich finde, Sie sollten dafür die Verantwortung übernehmen.
ish finduh zee zolten dafewr dee fairant-vortoong ewbernaymen

CONVERSIONS

inches

1 inch = 2.54 centimetres

metres

1 metre = 39.37 inches or 1.09 yards

kilometres

conversion: kilometres divided by 8, times 5 = miles

kilometres:	1	5	8	10	25	100
miles:	0.6	3.1	5	6.25	15.6	62.5

miles

conversion: miles divided by 5, times 8 = kilometres

miles:	1	3	5	10	20	100
kilometres:	1.6	4.8	8	16	32	160

kilos

conversion: kilos divided by 5, times 11 = pounds

kilos:	1	4	5	10	20	30	40
pounds:	2.2	8.8	11	22	44	66	88

pounds

1 pound = 0.45 kilos

conversion: pounds divided by 11, times 5 = kilos

litres

1 litre = approx. 1.75 pints or 0.22 gallons

Centigrade

conversion: C divided by 5, times 9, plus 32 = F

Centigrade:	10	18	25	28	30	34
Fahrenheit:	50	64	77	82	86	93

conversion: F minus 32, divided by 9, times 5 = C

DANCING AND DISCOS

Let's go to a disco.
Laß uns in eine Disco gehen.
lass oonss in īnuh disko gayen

Where can we go for ballroom dancing?
Wo können wir zu einem Tanzabend gehen?
vo kurnen veer tsoo īnem tantsahbent gayen

Do you want to dance?
Möchten Sie/möchtest du tanzen?
murshten zee/murshtest doo tantsen

Fancy another dance?
Noch einen Tanz?
noK īnen tants

I can't do the waltz.
Ich kann keinen Walzer tanzen.
ish kan kīnen valtser tantsen

Are you here by yourself?
Sind Sie/bist du allein hier?
zint zee/bist doo alīn heer

Great music.
Tolle Musik.
toluh moozeek

I can't hear you properly.
Ich kann Sie/dich schlecht verstehen.
ish kan zee/dish shlesht fairshtayen

Let's go to the bar.
Laß uns an die Bar gehen.
lass oonss an dee bar gayen

DAYS

Monday	Montag	*mohntahk*
Tuesday	Dienstag	*deenstahk*
Wednesday	Mittwoch	*mitvoK*
Thursday	Donnerstag	*donnerstahk*
Friday	Freitag	*frītahk*
Saturday	Samstag, Sonnabend	*zamstahk zonahbent*
Sunday	Sonntag	*zontahk*

On Monday.
Am Montag.
am mohntahk

On Tuesday evening.
Am Dienstag abend.
am deenstahk ahbent

On Saturdays.
Samstags.
zamstahks

On Saturday nights.
Samstag abends.
zamstahk ahbents

Yesterday.
Gestern.
gestern

Yesterday morning.
Gestern morgen.
gestern morgen

The day before yesterday.
Vorgestern.
forgestern

This afternoon.
Heute nachmittag.
hoytuh nahK-mittahk

Tomorrow.
Morgen.
morgen

Tomorrow afternoon.
Morgen nachmittag.
morgen nahK-mittahk

The day after tomorrow.
Übermorgen.
ewbermorgen

In the mornings.
Morgens.
morgens

In the evenings.
Abends.
ahbents

At nights.
Nachts.
nahKts

Next week.
Nächste Woche.
nexstuh voKuh

Every day.
Jeden Tag.
yayden tahk

DECLINING, SAYING NO

No thank you.
Nein, danke.
nīn dankuh

That's very kind, but no thanks.
Das ist sehr freundlich, aber danke nein.
*dass ist zair froyntlish **ah**ber dankuh nīn*

Thanks all the same though.
Trotzdem, vielen Dank.
trotsdaym feelen dank

I don't really want to.
Ich möchte eigentlich nicht.
*ish **mur**shtuh īgentlish nisht*

I don't really want one thanks.
Danke, ich möchte eigentlich keinen/keine/keins.
*dankuh ish **mur**shtuh īgentlish kīnen/kīnuh/kīnss*

Not for me/us thanks.
Für mich/uns nicht, danke.
fewr mish/oonss nisht dankuh

Not right now thanks.
Im Moment nicht, danke.
im moment nisht dankuh

No no, I'm not interested.
Nein danke, kein Interesse.
nīn dankuh kīn intressuh

I said no!
Ich sagte bereits, nein!
*ish **zah**gtuh berīts nīn*

DENTIST

I think I need a filling.
Ich glaube, ich brauche eine Füllung.
ish glowbuh ish browKuh īnuh fewloong

I've got/he's got a loose tooth.
Ich habe/er hat einen lockeren Zahn.
ish hahbuh/air hat īnen lockeren tsahn

I've got/she's got terrible toothache.
Ich habe/sie hat schreckliche Zahnschmerzen.
ish hahbuh/zee hat shrecklishuh tsahn-shmairtsen

Can you give me/him an injection?
Können Sie mir/ihm eine Spritze geben?
kurnen zee meer/eem īnuh shpritsuh gayben

What will it cost?
Was wird das kosten?
vass veert dass kosten

Could you write the cost down?
Könnten Sie die Kosten aufschreiben?
kurnten zee dee kosten owf-shrīben

Can you pull it out?
Können Sie ihn ziehen?
kurnen zee een tsee-en

Weit aufmachen.
vīt owf-mahKen
Open wide.

Er muß raus.
air mooss rowss
It'll have to come out.

Es wird nicht sehr weh tun.
ess veert nisht zair vay tOOn
This won't hurt much.

DIRECTIONS

Can you tell me the way to the station?
Wie komme ich bitte zum Bahnhof?
*vee kommuh ish bittuh tsoom **bahn**hohf*

I'm looking for Goethestraße.
Ich suche die Goethestraße.
*ish zOOKuh dee **gur**tuh-shtrahssuh*

Which is the best bus for getting to ...?
Mit welchem Bus fahre ich am besten nach ... ?
mit velshem booss faruh ish am besten nahK

Could you point it out on the map?
Könnten Sie es mir auf der Karte zeigen?
***kurn**ten zee ess meer owf dair **kar**tuh tsīgen*

Which road is it to Freiburg?
Welche Straße geht nach Freiburg?
***vel**shuh **shtrah**ssuh gayt nahK **frī**boork*

Is it near ...?
Ist es in der Nähe von ... ?
*ist ess in dair **nay**uh fon*

Excuse me, which street is this?
Entschuldigen Sie, welche Straße ist das hier?
*ent**shool**digen zee **vel**shuh **shtrah**ssuh ist dass heer*

How do I get there?
Wie komme ich dorthin?
*vee **kom**muh ish dort-**hin***

Is it walkable?
Kann ich das zu Fuß erreichen?
*kan ish dass tsOO fOOss air-**rī**shen*

Could you just point out the general direction?
Könnten Sie mir die grobe Richtung sagen?
***kurn**ten zee meer dee **groh**buh **rish**toong **zah**gen*

RESPONSES

Biegen Sie die erste Straße rechts ab.
*beegen zee dee **air**stuh shtr**ah**ssuh reshts ap*
Take the first right.

Biegen Sie die zweite Straße links ab.
*beegen zee dee tsvītuh shtr**ah**ssuh links ap*
Take the second left.

An der ersten Ampel links.
*an dair **air**sten **am**pel links*
Left at the first set of traffic lights.

Gehen/fahren Sie geradeaus.
*gayen/faren zee grahduh-**owss***
Go straight on.

Fahren Sie an der nächsten Ampel geradeaus.
*faren zee an dair nexsten **am**pel grahduh-**owss***
Go straight through the next lights.

An der Kirche/dem Museum rechts.
an dair keershuh/daym moozayoom reshts
Go right at the church/museum.

Gehen/fahren Sie über die Brücke.
gayen/faren zee ewber dee brewkuh
Go across the bridge.

Gehen/fahren Sie in dieser Richtung zurück bis . . .
gayen/faren zee in deezer rishtoong tsoorewk biss
Go back this way until . . .

Tut mir leid, ich bin auch fremd hier.
toot meer līt ish bin owk fremt heer
Sorry, I'm a stranger here myself.

DISAGREEING WITH PEOPLE

No, that's not right.
Nein, das stimmt nicht.
nīn dass shtimmt nisht

I don't think so.
Das glaube ich nicht.
dass glowbuh ish nisht

Oh no.
Aber nein.
ahber nīn

I think you're wrong.
Ich glaube, Sie irren sich.
ish glowbuh zee eerren zish

He's/they're wrong.
Er hat/sie haben unrecht.
air hat/zee hahben oonresht

I don't agree with that.
Ich bin anderer Meinung.
ish bin anderer mīnoong

Definitely not.
Ganz bestimmt nicht.
gants beshtimmt nisht

No way.
Auf keinen Fall.
owf kīnen fal

DISLIKES

I don't like beer/sauerkraut/this hotel.
Ich mag Bier/Sauerkraut/dieses Hotel nicht.
ish mahk beer/zowerkrowt/deezes hohtel nisht

I don't like swimming/playing tennis.
Ich gehe nicht gerne schwimmen/Tennis spielen.
ish gayuh nisht gairnuh shvimmen/tennis shpeelen

She doesn't like him.
Sie mag ihn nicht.
zee mahk een nisht

I don't like it.
Das gefällt mir nicht.
dass gefelt meer nisht

I don't like the look of that.
Das gefällt mir aber gar nicht.
dass gefelt meer ahber gar nisht

I can't stand . . .
Ich kann . . . nicht ausstehen
ish kan . . . nisht owss-shtayen

It doesn't taste very nice.
Das schmeckt nicht sehr gut.
dass shmeckt nisht zair gOOt

That's awful.
Das ist furchtbar.
dass ist fOOrshtbar

It was terrible.
Es war schrecklich.
ess var shrecklish

DOCTOR

Can you call a doctor?
Können Sie einen Arzt rufen?
kurnen zee īnen artst rOOfen

I'm a doctor/a nurse.
Ich bin Arzt/Krankenschwester.
ish bin artst/krankenshvester

He's had an accident.
Er hatte einen Unfall.
air hattuh īnen oonfal

I'm/he's/she's ill.
Ich bin/er ist/sie ist krank.
ish bin/air ist/zee ist krank

It's my stomach.
Es ist mein Magen.
ess ist mīn mahgen

It's my back.
Es ist mein Rücken.
ess ist mīn rewken

It's my chest.
Es ist mein Brustkorb.
ess ist mīn broostkorp

He/she fell over.
Er/sie ist hingefallen.
air/zee ist hin-gefal-en

I think it's broken.
Ich glaube, es ist gebrochen.
ish glowbuh ess ist gebroKen

He's/she's unconscious.
Er/sie ist bewußtlos.
air/zee ist bevoostlohss

It hurts here.
Es tut hier weh.
ess toot heer vay

It's a very sharp pain.
Es ist ein sehr stechender Schmerz.
ess ist īn zair shteshender shmairts

I've got insurance.
Ich bin versichert.
ish bin fairzishert

What will it cost?
Was wird das kosten?
vass veert dass kosten

RESPONSES

Es ist nichts Ernstes.
ess ist nishts airnstes
It's nothing serious.

Sie müssen/er muß ins Krankenhaus.
zee mewssen/air mooss inss krankenhowss
You'll/he'll have to come/go into hospital.

Sie müssen/sie muß operiert werden.
zee mewssen/zee mooss oper-reert vairden
You'll/she'll need an operation.

Es ist eine Blinddarmentzündung.
ess ist īnuh blint-darm-ent-tsewndoong
It's appendicitis.

Es ist gebrochen.
ess ist gebroKen
It's broken.

Es ist ein Herzanfall.
ess ist īn hairts-anfal
It's a heart attack.

Es ist eine Lebensmittelvergiftung.
ess ist īnuh laybens-mittel-fair-giftoong
It's food poisoning.

Gehen Sie hiermit zur Apotheke.
gayen zee heermit tsoor apotaykuh
Take this to a chemist.

DRINKS

What are you drinking?
Was möchten Sie/möchtest du trinken?
vass murshten zee/murshtest doo trinken

A cup of coffee/a tea please.
Eine Tasse Kaffee/einen Tee, bitte.
īnuh tassuh kafay/īnen tay bittuh

Two coffees and a beer.
Zwei Kaffee und ein Bier.
tsvī kafay oont īn beer

Two white wines please.
Zwei Gläser Weißwein, bitte.
tsvī glayzer vīssvīn bittuh

A litre carafe of red wine.
Einen Liter Rotwein.
īnen leeter rohtvīn

Dry wine/sweet wine/medium dry wine.
Trockener Wein/süßer Wein/halbtrockener Wein.
trockener vīn/sewsser vīn/halp-trockener vīn

The same again please.
Das gleiche noch einmal, bitte.
dass glīshuh noK īnmal bittuh

No ice for me thanks.
Für mich kein Eis, danke.
fewr mish kīn īss dankuh

I'd rather have draught beer.
Ich hätte lieber Bier vom Faß.
ish hettuh leeber beer fom fass

It's my/your round.
Ich gebe/du gibst einen aus.
ish gaybuh/doo geepst īnen owss

DRINKS LIST

das Alsterwasser *alstervasser* shandy
das Altbier *altbeer* dark beer
der Apfelsaft *apfelzaft* apple juice
der Apfelwein *apfelvīn* cider
der Äppelwoi *epelvoy* cider
die Auslese *owss-layzuh* wine from quality grapes
die Berliner Weiße mit Schuß *bairleener vīssuh mit shooss* light beer with a dash of raspberry etc juice
das Bier *beer* beer
das Bockbier *bockbeer* strong sweet dark beer
die Bowle *bohluh* punch
die Eisschokolade *īss-shokolahduh* cold chocolate with ice cream
der Federweiße *faydervīssuh* new wine, still fermenting
der Fruchtsaft *frooKtzaft* fruit juice
der Glühwein *glewvīn* mulled wine
die heiße Schokolade *hīssuh shokolahduh* hot chocolate
der Heurige *hoyriguh* new wine, still fermenting
der Kakao *kakow* cocoa
das Kännchen Kaffee *kenshen kafay* pot of coffee
der Korn *korn* type of schnapps
der Likör *likur* liqueur
das Malzbier *maltsbeer* malt beer
die Maß *mahss* litre of beer
die Milch *milsh* milk
der Orangensaft *oronjenzaft* orange juice
der Radler *rahdler* shandy
der Rotwein *rohtvīn* red wine
die Schorle *shorluh* wine with lemonade
der Sekt *zekt* sparkling wine
das Selterswasser *zeltersvasser* mineral water
das Spezi *shpaytsee* coke and lemonade
das Sprudelwasser *shprOOdelvasser* mineral water
das Tafelwasser *tahfelvasser* still mineral water
der Tafelwein *tahfelvīn* table wine
die Tasse Tee *tassuh tay* cup of tea
der Underberg (*tm*) *oonderbairk* digestif
vom Faß *fom fass* draught
der Weinbrand *vīnbrant* brandy
der Weißwein *vīssvīn* white wine
das Weizenbier *vītsenbeer* light beer

DRIVING

(*see also* *CAR ACCIDENTS, GARAGE, RENTALS*)

Can I park here?
Kann ich hier parken?
kan ish heer parken

Where can I park the car?
Wo kann ich parken?
vo kan ish parken

Where is the nearest petrol station?
Wo ist die nächste Tankstelle?
vo ist dee nexstuh tank-shtelluh

Is this the road for . . . ?
Ist dies die Straße nach . . . ?
ist deess dee shtrahssuh nahK

We came by car.
Wir sind mit dem Auto gekommen.
veer zint mit daym owto gekommen

We're going to drive to . . .
Wir fahren nach . . .
veer faren nahK

How long does it take to drive there?
Wie lange fährt man dorthin?
vee lang-uh fayrt man dort-hin

It's in the car.
Es ist im Auto.
ess ist im owto

Let's take my car.
Wollen wir meinen Wagen nehmen?
vollen veer mīnen vahgen naymen

EMERGENCIES

(*see also THEFT*)

I'm lost.
Ich habe mich verirrt.
*ish **hah**buh mish faireerrt*

It's broken.
Es ist kaputt.
*ess ist ka**poot***

It's stuck.
Es sitzt fest.
ess zitst fest

Help!
Hilfe!
***hil**fuh*

Call the police!
Rufen Sie die Polizei!
rOO**fen zee dee po**litsī

There's a fire!
Es brennt!
ess brent

The tap won't turn off.
Der Wasserhahn läßt sich nicht zudrehen.
*dair **vass**erhahn lest zish nisht **tsOO**drayen*

There's a smell of gas.
Es riecht nach Gas.
ess reesht nahK gahss

The toilet won't flush.
Die Toilette spült nicht.
*dee twa**let**tuh shpewlt nisht*

The ... gives you an electric shock.
Von dem/der . . . bekommt man einen elektrischen Schlag.
fon daym/dair . . . bekommt man īnen elektrishen shlahg

Get a doctor!
Holen Sie einen Arzt!
hohlen zee īnen artst

He's had an accident.
Er hatte einen Unfall.
air hattuh īnen oonfal

It's very urgent.
Es ist sehr dringend.
ess ist zair dring-ent

I've locked myself out.
Ich habe mich ausgesperrt.
ish hahbuh mish owss-geshpairt

This man is pestering me.
Dieser Mann belästigt mich.
deezer man belestikt mish

Does anyone speak English?
Spricht hier jemand Englisch?
shprisht heer yaymant eng-lish

EXPLAINING THINGS

(*see also INTENTIONS*)

It's necessary to . . .
Man muß . . .
man mooss

You have to push this button.
Man muß auf diesen Knopf drücken.
man mooss owf deezen k-nopf drewken

It's because of . . .
Das ist wegen . . .
dass ist vaygen

You need . . .
Man braucht . . .
man browKt

I didn't know that.
Das wußte ich nicht.
dass voostuh ish nisht

It wasn't possible to . . .
Man konnte nicht . . .
man kontuh nisht

She didn't understand you, that's why.
Sie hat Sie nicht verstanden, deshalb.
zee hat zee nisht fairshtanden dess-halp

If you . . . then . . .
Wenn Sie . . . dann . . .
ven zee . . . dan

I'll get an interpreter.
Ich hole einen Dolmetscher.
ish hohluh inen dolmetsher

FEEL: HOW YOU FEEL

I'm/he's hungry.
Ich habe/er hat Hunger.
ish hahbuh/air hat hoong-er

I'm/we're thirsty.
Ich habe/wir haben Durst.
ish hahbuh/veer hahben doorst

I'm/she's tired.
Ich bin/sie ist müde.
ish bin/zee ist mewduh

I'm/he's bored.
Ich habe/er hat Langeweile.
ish hahbuh/air hat lang-uh-vīluh

I'm/they're sleepy.
Ich schlafe/sie schlafen gleich ein.
ish shlahfuh/zee shlahfen glīsh īn

I feel fine thanks.
Mir geht es gut, danke.
meer gayt ess gOOt dankuh

I feel great!
Ich fühle mich prima!
ish fewluh mish preema

I feel much better.
Es geht mir viel besser.
ess gayt meer feel besser

He's much better thanks.
Es geht ihm viel besser, danke.
ess gayt eem feel besser dankuh

How are you feeling?
Wie fühlen Sie sich?
vee fewlen zee zish

FLYING

Can you take us to the airport?
Können Sie uns zum Flughafen bringen?
kurnen zee oonss tsoom flOOk-hahfen bring-en

Where does the airport bus stop?
Wo hält der Flughafenbus?
vo helt dair flOOk-hahfenbooss

Is this ok for the airport?
Fährt der zum Flughafen?
fayrt dair tsoom flOOk-hahfen

I'd like a single/return to . . .
Ich hätte gern ein einfaches Ticket/ein Rückflugticket nach . . .
ish hettuh gairn īn īnfahKes ticket/īn rewk-flOOkticket nahK

Non-smoking, please.
Nichtraucher, bitte.
nisht-rowKer bittuh

Smoking, please.
Raucher, bitte.
rowKer bittuh

A window seat if possible.
Einen Fensterplatz, wenn möglich.
īnen fensterplats ven murglish

Which gate is it?
Welcher Flugsteig ist es?
velsher flOOk-shtīk ist ess?

What time is the next flight?
Wann geht der nächste Flug?
van gayt dair nexstuh flOOk

FORBIDDING

You mustn't . . .
Sie dürfen/du darfst nicht . . .
zee dewrfen/dOO darfst nisht

You shouldn't do that.
Das sollten Sie/solltest du nicht machen.
dass zolten zee/zoltest dOO nisht mahKen

Don't do that.
Lassen Sie/laß das sein.
lassen zee/lass dass zīn

Don't do anything until I say so.
Machen Sie nichts bis ich es sage.
mahKen zee nishts biss ish ess zahguh

He's not to . . .
Er soll nicht . . .
air zol nisht

That's not allowed.
Das ist nicht erlaubt.
dass ist nisht airlowpt

No way!
Auf keinen Fall!
owf kīnen fal

Stop that right now!
Hören Sie sofort damit auf!
huren zee zofort damit owf

Verboten
fairbohten
Forbidden.

Untersagt.
oonterzahgt
Prohibited.

FUTURE

To talk about what is going to happen in the future you can very often use the present tense (*see PRESENT*). English works in a similar way, for example:

Our train leaves at 11.00 tomorrow.
Unser Zug fährt morgen um elf Uhr.
oonzer tsOOk fairt morgen oom elf OOr

I'm going home next week.
Ich fahre nächste Woche nach Hause.
ish faruh nexstuh voKuh nahK howzuh

German often uses the present tense where English uses the future:

I'll be right back.
Ich bin gleich zurück.
ish bin glīsh tsOOrewk

I'll do it straight away.
Ich mache es sofort.
ish mahKuh ess zofort

The actual future tense in German, used to say 'I will, you will' etc is formed by taking the verb as given in the dictionary section of this book and placing the following words in front of it:

I will speak	**ich WERDE sprechen** *(vairduh)*
you will speak	**Sie WERDEN sprechen** *(vairden)*
(fam. singular)	**du WIRST sprechen** *(veerst)*
he/she/it will speak	**er/sie/es WIRD sprechen** *(veert)*
we will speak	**wir WERDEN sprechen** *(vairden)*
you will speak	**Sie WERDEN sprechen**
(fam plural)	**ihr WERDET sprechen** *(vairdet)*
they will speak	**sie WERDEN sprechen**

Here are some examples:

It won't be easy.
Es wird nicht leicht sein.
ess veert nisht līsht zīn

Will it be ready by tomorrow?
Wird das bis morgen fertig sein?
veert dass biss morgen fairtik zīn

We shall see.
Wir werden sehen.
veer vairden zayen

What are you going to do?
Was werden Sie/wirst du machen?
vass vairden zee/veerst doo maKen

GARAGES

(*see also DRIVING*)

30 litres of this type please.
30 Liter von dieser Sorte, bitte.
drissik leeter fon deezer zortuh bittuh

Could you fill it up?
Könnten Sie bitte volltanken?
kurnten zee bittuh fol-tanken

1 litre of oil please.
Einen Liter Öl, bitte.
inen leeter url bittuh

Do you do repairs?
Machen Sie Reparaturen?
mahKen zee reparatOOren

Could you have a look at the front brakes?
Könnten Sie sich mal die vorderen Bremsen ansehen?
kurnten zee zish mal dee forderen bremzen an-zayen

I think there's something wrong with the brakes/clutch.
Ich glaube, mit den Bremsen/der Kupplung stimmt was nicht.
ish glowbuh mit dayn bremzen/dair kooploong shtimmt vass nisht

It's losing water.
Er verliert Kühlwasser.
air fairleert kewlvasser

It's overheating.
Er läuft heiß.
air loyft hiss

It keeps cutting out.
Er geht immer wieder aus.
air gayt immer veeder owss

It takes a long time to start.
Es dauert lange, bis er anspringt.
ess dowert lang-uh biss air an-shpringt

The steering is slack.
Die Lenkung ist lose.
dee lenkoong ist lohzuh

The door won't lock.
Die Tür läßt sich nicht abschließen.
dee tewr lest zish nisht ap-shleessen

The lights are faulty.
Die Scheinwerfer sind defekt.
dee shīn-vairfer zint dayfekt

I need a new indicator bulb.
Ich brauche eine neue Blinklichtbirne.
ish browKuh īnuh noyuh blink-lisht-beernuh

Can you do it now?
Können Sie es sofort machen?
kurnen zee ess zofort mahKen

Can you do it today?
Können Sie es heute noch machen?
kurnren zee ess hoytuh noK mahKen

When can I pick it up?
Wann kann ich ihn abholen?
van kan ish een ap-hohlen

WEST GERMANY

A country of widely varying scenery, from the Alps in the south to plains in the north, with deep river valleys and thick extensive forests, West Germany has a population of 61.1 million living in an area of some 246,000 square kilometres (as compared to the UK's 56 million in 244,000 square kilometres). Some basic facts and figures:

The largest cities are Berlin (West) with a population of 1.86m, Hamburg with 1.61m, Munich (München) with 1.28m and Cologne (Köln) which has 0.94m.

There are considerable differences of accent between Germans from the north and those from the south.

The longest rivers are the Rhine (der Rhein) which is 865 km long, the Moselle (die Mosel) which is 647 km, the Danube (die Donau) at 647 km, the Main at 524 km, the Weser at 440 km and the Elbe at 227 km.

The seat of the West German government is in Bonn, which is the federal capital. The country is divided up into 11 states, known as **Länder** *lender*, each of which has its own capital city:

	capital
Baden-Württemberg	Stuttgart
Bayern (Bavaria)	München (Munich)
Berlin (West)	Berlin
Bremen	Bremen
Hamburg	Hamburg
Hessen	Wiesbaden
Niedersachsen (Lower Saxony)	Hannover
Nordrhein-Westfalen	Düsseldorf
Rheinland-Pfalz	Mainz
Saarland	Saarbrücken
Schleswig-Holstein	Kiel

HAIRDRESSER

Just a trim please.
Nur nachschneiden, bitte.
noor nahK-shnīden bittuh

Could you take about 2 inches off all round?
Könnten Sie bitte überall 5 Zentimeter abschneiden?
kurnten zee bittuh ewberal fewnf tsentimayter ap-shnīden

Could you tidy up the ends?
Könnten Sie die Spitzen begradigen?
kurnten zee dee shpitsen begrahdigen

Not too short.
Nicht zu kurz.
nisht tsoo koorts

Could you thin it out a bit?
Könnten Sie es etwas ausdünnen?
kurnten zee ess etvass owss-dewnnen

On top.
Oben.
ohben

At the sides.
An den Seiten.
an dayn zīten

I'd like it a lot shorter.
Ich hätte es gerne sehr viel kürzer.
ish hettuh ess gairnuh zair feel kewrtser

Up to about here.
Ungefähr bis hier.
oon-gefayr biss heer

Just over the ears.
Knapp über den Ohren.
k-nap ewber dayn orren

A shampoo and set please.
Waschen und legen, bitte.
vashen oont laygen bittuh

Can you put highlights in?
Können Sie mir Strähnchen machen?
kurnen zee meer shtrayn-shen mahKen

Can you do my roots?
Können Sie den dunklen Haaransatz überfärben?
kurnen zee dayn doonklen haransats ewber-fairben

Can you give me a perm?
Können Sie mir eine Dauerwelle machen?
kurnen zee meer īnuh dower-veluh mahKen

Tight curls/loose curls.
Feste Locken/weiche Locken.
festuh locken/vīshuh locken

RESPONSES

Möchten Sie eine Haarkur?
murshten zee īnuh harkOOr
Would you like conditioner?

Föhnen?
furnen
A blow dry?

HELLO – GOODBYE

Hello.
Guten Tag; (*in the evening*) guten Abend.
gOOten tahk, gOOten ahbent

Hi there.
Hallo.
hallo

Goodbye.
Auf Wiedersehen.
owf veederzayen

Cheerio.
Tschüs.
chewss

See you later.
Bis später.
biss shpayter

Good morning/good afternoon/good evening.
Guten Morgen/guten Tag/guten Abend.
gOOten morgen/gOOten tahk/gOOten ahbent

Good night.
Gute Nacht.
gOOtuh nahKt

Pleased to meet you.
Freut mich.
froyt mish

It was nice meeting you.
Es war nett, Sie kennenzulernen.
ess var net zee kenen-tsOO-lairnen

HITCH-HIKING

Are you going to . . .?
Fahren Sie nach . . .?
faren zee nahK

Are you going anywhere near . . .?
Fahren Sie in die Nähe von . . .?
faren zee in dee nayuh fon

Can you give me/us a lift?
Können Sie mich/uns mitnehmen?
kurnen zee mish/oonss mitnaymen

We've been standing here for two hours.
Wir stehen schon seit zwei Stunden hier.
veer shtayen shohn zīt tsvī shtoonden heer

Do you have room for four people?
Haben Sie Platz für vier Leute?
hahben zee plats fewr veer loytuh

Can you drop us off here/at the next services?
Können Sie uns hier/an der nächsten Raststätte absetzen?
kurnen zee oons heer/an dair nexsten rast-shtettuh ap-zetsen

That's very kind of you.
Das ist sehr freundlich von Ihnen.
dass ist zair froyntlish fon eenen

RESPONSES

Wohin wollen Sie?
vohin vollen zee
Where are you going?

Ich fahre nur bis . . .
ish faruh nOOr biss
I'm only going as far as . . .

HOSPITAL

(*see also DOCTOR*)

Can you take us to the hospital?
Können Sie uns zum Krankenhaus bringen?
kurnen zee oonss tsoom krankenhowss bring-en

To the casualty department.
Zur Unfallstation.
tsOOr oonfal-shtats-yohn

To the maternity unit.
Zur Entbindungsstation.
tsOOr entbindoongs-shtats-yohn

Which ward is he/she in?
Auf welcher Station ist er/sie?
owf velsher shtats-yohn ist air/zee

How is he/she doing?
Wie geht es ihm/ihr?
vee gayt ess eem/eer

> **Besser/nicht sehr gut.**
> *besser/nisht zair gOOt*
> Better/not very well.

When are visiting hours?
Wann ist Besuchszeit?
van ist bezOOKs-tsīt

How long will I/he have to stay in for?
Wie lange muß ich/er dableiben?
vee lang-uh mooss ish/air da-blīben

Is treatment covered by this insurance?
Wird die Behandlung von dieser Versicherung getragen?
veert dee behantloong fon deezer fair-zisheroong getrahgen

HOTELS

(*see also ROOMS, SELF-CATERING*)

Do you have a room for one night?
Haben Sie ein Zimmer für eine Nacht?
hahben zee īn tsimmer fewr īnuh nahKt

For two nights/for a week.
Für zwei Nächte/für eine Woche.
fewr tsvī neshtuh/fewr īnuh voKuh

Do you have a single room/double room?
Haben Sie ein Einzelzimmer/Doppelzimmer?
hahben zee īn īntsel-tsimmer/doppel-tsimmer

For two people/for two adults and one child.
Für zwei Personen/für zwei Erwachsene und ein Kind.
fewr tsvī pairzohnen/fewr tsvī airvaksenuh oont īn kint

I have a reservation.
Ich habe reserviert.
ish hahbuh rezerveert

How much is it per night?
Wieviel kostet es pro Nacht?
veefeel kostet ess pro nahKt

Could you write the cost down?
Könnten Sie die Kosten aufschreiben?
kurnten zee dee kosten owf-shrīben

We'd like a room with two single beds.
Wir hätten gerne ein Zimmer mit zwei Einzelbetten.
veer hetten gairnuh īn tsimmer mit tsvī īntsel-betten

We'd like a room with a double bed.
Wir hätten gerne ein Zimmer mit einem Doppelbett.
veer hetten gairnuh īn tsimmer mit īnem doppel-bet

Can we see the room?
Können wir das Zimmer sehen?
kurnen veer dass tsimmer zayen

RESPONSES

Für wie lange?
fewr vee lang-uh
For how long?

Ihr Name, bitte?
eer nahmuh bittuh
Your name please?

Kann ich Ihren Paß sehen?
kan ish eeren pas zayen
Can I see your passport?

Wie möchten Sie bezahlen?
vee murshten zee betsahlen
How will you be paying?

By credit card/cash.
Mit Kreditkarte/in bar.
mit kredeetkartuh/in bar

Can I have the bill for room 220 please?
Kann ich bitte die Rechnung für Zimmer 220 haben?
kan ish bittuh dee reshnoong fewr tsimmer tsvī-hoondert-tsvantsik hahben

I'd like to stay another night.
Ich möchte gerne noch eine Nacht bleiben.
ish murshtuh gairnuh noK īnuh nahKt blīben

Another two nights.
Noch zwei Nächte.
noK tsvī neshtuh

Es gießt wie aus Eimern.
ess geest vee owss īmern
It's raining cats and dogs.

Sie wollen mich wohl auf den Arm nehmen?
zee vollen mish vohl owf dayn arm naymen
Are you pulling my leg?

Das ist nicht mein Fall.
dass ist nisht mīn fal
It's not my cup of tea.

Ich habe geschlafen wie ein Bär.
ish hahbuh geshlahfen vee īn bair
I slept like a log.

Er raucht wie ein Schlot.
air rowKt vee īn shloht
He smokes like a chimney.

Das ist ein Kinderspiel.
dass ist īn kinder-shpeel
That's child's play.

Das ist nur ein Katzensprung.
dass ist nOOr īn katsen-shproong
It's only a stone's throw away.

Das ist jwd.
dass ist jot-vay-day
That's at the back of beyond.

Jetzt geht es um die Wurst!
yetst gayt ess oom dee voorst
It's now or never!

INTENTIONS

What are you going to do?
Was werden Sie machen?
vass vairden zee mahKen

I'll be back soon.
Ich bin gleich zurück.
ish bin glīsh tsOOrewk

I'll bring it back this afternoon.
Ich bringe es heute nachmittag zurück.
ish bring-uh ess hoytuh nahK-mittahk tsOOrewk

I'll go to the bank and then come back with the money.
Ich gehe zur Bank und komme dann mit dem Geld zurück.
ish gayuh tsOOr bank oont kommuh dan mit daym gelt tsOOrewk

I'll give it to him for you.
Ich werde es ihm von Ihnen geben.
ish vairduh ess eem fon eenen gayben

I'll leave this here as a deposit.
Ich lasse dies als Anzahlung hier.
ish lassuh deess alss antsahloong heer

I'm coming back next week.
Ich komme nächste Woche wieder.
ish kommuh nexstuh voKuh veeder

I'll do something about it, I promise.
Ich verspreche, daß ich mich darum kümmern werde.
ish fairshpreshuh dass ish mish daroom kewmern vairduh

I'll go and get . . .
Ich gehe . . . holen.
ish gayuh . . . hohlen

INVITING PEOPLE

Would you like to . . .?
Möchten Sie/möchtest du . . .?
murshten zee/murshtest doo

Would you like to come with us?
Möchten Sie mit uns kommen?
murshten zee mit oonss kommen

Would you like to have a drink?
Möchten Sie etwas trinken?
murshten zee etvass trinken

Would you like to come out this evening?
Möchten Sie heute abend ausgehen?
murshten zee hoytuh ahbent owss-gayen

What are you doing tonight?
Was machen Sie/machst du heute abend?
vass mahKen zee/mahKst doo hoytuh ahbent

How about a meal this evening?
Wollen wir heute abend essen gehen?
vollen veer hoytuh ahbent essen gayen

We'd like to invite you out.
Wir möchten Sie gerne zum Ausgehen einladen.
veer murshten zee gairnuh tsoom owss-gayen īn-lahden

Thanks for the invitation, but . . .
Vielen Dank für die Einladung, aber . . .
feelen dank fewr dee īn-lahdoong ahber

LIKES

I like this wine.
Ich mag diesen Wein.
ish mahk deezen vīn

I like sausages a lot.
Ich mag Würstchen sehr gerne.
ish mahk vewrst-shen zair gairnuh

I like swimming/walking.
Ich gehe gerne schwimmen/spazieren.
ish gayuh gairnuh shvimmen/shpatseeren

She likes him.
Sie mag ihn.
zee mahk een

I like it.
Das gefällt mir.
dass gefelt meer

I like it here.
Es gefällt mir hier.
ess gefelt meer heer

I love you/this beer/these colours.
Ich liebe dich/dieses Bier/diese Farben.
ish leebuh dish/deezess beer/deezuh farben

It's beautiful. (food etc)
Es ist wunderbar.
ess ist voonderbar

It was fantastic.
Es war fantastisch.
ess var fantastish

MAP

DEN.
Kiel
Hamburg
Bremen
GERMAN
DEM.
REP.
POLAND
HOLL.
Hannover
Berlin
Dortmund
Cologne (Köln)
Leipzig
Dresden
BELG.
Bonn
LUX.
Frankfurt
Prague
GERMAN FEDERAL
REPUBLIC
CZECHOSLOVAKIA
Nuremberg
(Nürnberg)
Stuttgart
FRANCE
Linz
Vienna
(Wien)
Munich
(München)
AUSTRIA
Zurich
Innsbruck
Graz
SWITZ.
ITALY

MENU READER

Aal, grün *ahl grewn* eel, fresh
Am Spieß *am shpeess* on the spit
Ananas *ananass* pineapple
Apfel im Schlafrock *apfel im shlahfrock* baked apples in puff pastry
Apfelsinen *apfelzeenen* oranges
Apfeltasche *apfeltashuh* apple turnover
Auflauf *owflowf* (baked) pudding or omelette
Aufschnitt *owf-shnit* sliced cold meats
Austern *owstern* oysters

Baiser *bayzay* meringue
Balkansalat *balkahn-zalaht* cabbage and pepper salad
Bauernfrühstück *bowern-frewshtewk* bacon and potato omelette
Bechamelsauce *bayshamel-zohssuh* creamy sauce with onions and ham
Beilagen *bīlahgen* side dishes
Birnen *beernen* pears
Biskuit *beess-kveet* sponge
Bismarckheringe *bissmark-hayring-uh* filleted pickled herrings
Blätterteig *bletter-tīk* puff pastry
Blau *blow* au bleu, boiled
Blumenkohl *bloomen-kohl* cauliflower
Blutwurst *bloot-voorst* black pudding
Bockwurst *bock-voorst* large frankfurter
Bohnen *bohnen* beans
Bouillon *bool-yohn* clear soup
Bouletten *booletten* meatballs
Brat- *braht* fried
Braten *brahten* roast meat
Bratkartoffeln *braht-kartoffeln* fried potatoes
Brot *broht* bread
Brühwurst *brew-voorst* large frankfurter
Brust *broost* breast
Bückling *bewkling* smoked red herring
Buttercremetorte *bootter-kraym-tortuh* cream cake

Champignons *shampeen-yonss* mushrooms

Chinakohl *sheena-kohl* Chinese leaves
Currywurst *kuree-voorst* curried pork sausage

Deutsches Beefsteak *doytchess 'beefsteak'* minced meat steak
Dicke Bohnen *dickuh bohnen* broad beans

Eier *ī-er* eggs
Eintopf *īntopf* stew
Eis *īss* ice, ice cream
Eisbecher *īss-besher* sundae
Eisbein *īss-bīn* knuckles of pork
Entenbraten *enten-brahten* roast duck
Erbsen *airpsen* peas
Erdbeertorte *airt-bair-tortuh* strawberry cake
Essig *essik* vinegar

Fasan *fazahn* pheasant
Feldsalat *felt-zalaht* lamb's lettuce
Fisch *fish* fish
Fischstäbchen *fish-shtaybshen* fish fingers
Fleischkäse *flīsh-kayzuh* meat loaf
Fleischwurst *flīsh-voorst* pork sausage
Forelle Müllerin (Art) *forelluh mewllerin (art)* trout with butter and lemon (breaded)
Frikadelle *frikadelluh* rissole
Frühlingsrolle *frewlings-rolluh* spring roll

Gänsebraten *genzuh-brahten* roast goose
Gebacken *gebacken* fried
Gebraten *gebrahten* roast
Gedünstet *gedewnstet* steamed
Geflügel *geflewgel* poultry
Gefüllt *gefewlt* stuffed
Gekocht *gekoKt* boiled
Gemüse *gemewzuh* vegetable(s)
Geräuchert *geroyshert* smoked
Gericht *gerisht* dish
Geschnetzeltes *geshnetseltess* strips of meat in thick sauce

Gespickt mit . . . *geshpickt mit* larded with . . .
Goldbarsch *goltbarsh* type of perch
Grieß *greess* semolina
Grünkohl *grewnkohl* (curly) kale
Gurkensalat *goorken-zalaht* cucumber salad

Hackfleisch *hack-flīsh* mince
Hähnchen *haynshen* chicken
Hammelfleisch *hammel-flīsh* mutton
Hauptspeisen *howpt-shpīzen* main courses
Hausmacher (Art) *howss-mahKer (art)* home-made-style
Heidelbeeren *hīdelbayren* bilberries, blueberries
Heringstopf *hayrings-topf* pickled herrings in sauce
Himbeeren *himbayren* raspberries
Himmel und Erde *himmel oont airduh* potato and apple purée with blood/liver sausage
Hoppelpoppel *hoppel-poppel* bacon and potato omelette
Hühnerbrühe *hewner-brewuh* clear chicken soup
Hühnerfrikassee *hewner-freekassay* chicken fricassée

Jägerschnitzel *jayger-shnitsel* cutlet with mushrooms

Kabeljau *kahbel-yow* cod
Kaiserschmarren *kīzer-shmarren* sugared pancake with raisins
Kalbfleisch *kalp-flīsh* veal
Kalte Platte *kaltuh plattuh* salad
Kaltschale *kalt-shahluh* cold sweet soup
Kaninchen *kaneenshen* rabbit
Karpfen *karpfen* carp
Kartoffelbrei *kartoffelbrī* potato purée
Kartoffelpuffer *kartoffel-pooffer* potato fritters
Käse *kayzuh* cheese
Käse-Sahne-Torte *kayzuh-zahnuh-tortuh* cream cheesecake
Kassler *kassler* smoked and braised pork chop
Katenleberwurst *kahtenlayber-voorst* smoked liver pâté
Keule *koyluh* leg, haunch
Kirschen *keershen* cherries
Klare Brühe *klahruh brewuh* clear soup

Klöße *klurssuh* dumplings
Knacker *k-nacker* frankfurter(s)
Knoblauch *k-nohblowK* garlic
Knochen *k-noKen* bone
Knödel *k-nurdel* dumplings
Kohl *kohl* cabbage
Kohl und Pinkel *kohl oont pinkel* cabbage, potatoes, sausage and smoked meat
Kohlrouladen *kohl-rOOlahden* stuffed cabbage leaves
Kompott *kompott* stewed fruit
Königsberger Klopse *kurniks-bairger klopsuh* meatballs in caper sauce
Kopfsalat *kopf-zalaht* lettuce
Kotelett *kotlet* cutlet
Krabben *krabben* shrimps/prawns
Kräuter *kroyter* herbs
Krautsalat *krowt-zalaht* coleslaw
Kuchen *kOOKen* cake

Labskaus *lapskowss* meat, fish and potato stew
Lachs *laks* salmon
Lachsschinken *laks-shinken* smoked rolled fillet of ham
Lamm *lam* lamb
Lauchsuppe *lowK-zoopuh* leek soup
Leberkäse *layber-kayzuh* baked pork and beef loaf
Leberpastete *layber-pastaytuh* liver pâté
Leberwurst *layber-voorst* liver pâté
Leipziger Allerlei *līptsiger al-erlī* mixed vegetables
Linsensuppe *linzen-zoopuh* lentil soup

Mager *mahger* lean
Markklößchen *mark-klurss-shen* marrow dumplings
Marmorkuchen *marmor-kOOKen* marble cake
Matjes(hering) *mat-yess(-hayring)* young herring
Medaillons *medī-yonss* small fillets
Meeresfrüchte *mayress-frewshtuh* seafood
Meerrettich *mayrettish* horseradish
Milchreis *milsh-rīss* rice pudding
Möhren *murren* carrots
Mus *mOOss* purée

Muscheln *moosheln* mussels
Muskat(nuß) *mooskaht(nooss)* nutmeg

Nach Art des Hauses *nahK art dess howzess* à la maison
Nachtisch *nahKtish* dessert
Nüsse *newssuh* nuts

Obstsalat *ohpst-zalaht* fruit salad
Ochsenschwanzsuppe *okzen-shvants-zoopuh* oxtail soup

Palatschinken *palaht-shinken* stuffed pancakes
Paniert *paneert* with breadcrumbs
Paprikaschoten *papreeka-shohten* peppers
Pastete *pastaytuh* vol-au-vent
Pellkartoffeln *pelkartoffeln* potatoes boiled in their jackets
Petersilie *payterzeel-yuh* parsley
Pfannkuchen *pfan-kooKen* pancake(s)
Pfeffer *pfeffer* pepper
Pfifferlinge *pfifferling-uh* chanterelles
Pfirsiche *pfeerzishuh* peaches
Pflaumen *pflowmen* plums
Pichelsteiner Topf *pishel-shtīner topf* vegetable stew with diced beef
Pikant *peekant* spicy
Pilze *piltsuh* mushrooms
Platte *plattuh* selection
Pökelfleisch *purkel-flīsh* salt meat
Pommes frites *pom-frit* French fried potatoes
Porree *porray* leek
Preiselbeeren *prīzelbayren* cranberries
Pumpernickel *poompernickel* black rye bread
Puter *pooter* turkey

Quark *kvark* curd cheese

Rahm *rahm* (sour) cream
Rehbraten *raybrahten* roast venison

Reibekuchen *ribuh-kooKen* potato waffles
Reis *riss* rice
Rinderrouladen *rinder-rOOlahden* stuffed beef rolls
Rindfleisch *rint-flish* beef
Rippchen *ripshen* spare-ribs
Risi-Pisi *reezee-peezee* rice and peas
Roh *ro* raw
Rohkostplatte *ro-kost-plattuh* selection of salads
Rosenkohl *rohzen-kohl* Brussels sprouts
Rosinen *rohzeenen* raisins
Rotbarsch *rohtbarsh* type of perch
Rote Bete *rohtuh baytuh* beetroot
Rotkohl *roht-kohl* red cabbage
Rühreier *rewr-ī-er* scrambled eggs
Russische Eier *roossishuh ī-er* egg mayonnaise

Sahne *zahnuh* cream
Salz *zalts* salt
Salzburger Nockerln *zalts-boorger nockerln* dumplings
Salzheringe *zalts-hayring-uh* salted herrings
Salzkartoffeln *zalts-kartoffeln* boiled potatoes
Sauerbraten *zower-brahten* marinaded pot roast
Sauerkraut *zower-krowt* white cabbage, finely chopped and pickled
Schaschlik *shashlik* (shish-)kebab
Schattenmorellen *shatten-mohrellen* morello cherries
Schellfisch *shellfish* haddock
Schildkrötensuppe *shiltkrurten-zoopuh* real turtle soup
Schillerlocken *shillerlocken* smoked haddock rolls
Schinken *shinken* ham
Schlachtplatte *shlaKt-plattuh* selection of fresh sausages
Schlagsahne *shlahk-zahnuh* whipped cream
Schmorbraten *shmorbrahten* pot roast
Schnittlauch *shnitlowK* chives
Schnitzel *shnitsel* cutlet
Scholle *sholluh* plaice
Schwarzbrot *shvarts-broht* brown rye bread
Schwarzwälder Kirschtorte *shvartsvelder keersh-tortuh* Black Forest cherry gateau
Schwarzwurzeln *shvarts-voortseln* salsifies
Schweinefleisch *shvīnuh-flīsh* pork

Schweinshaxe *shvīns-haksuh* knuckle of pork
Seelachs *zaylaks* type of cod
Seezunge *zaytsoong-uh* sole
Sellerie *zelleree* celery, celeriac
Semmelknödel *zemmel-k-nurdel* bread dumplings
Senf *zenf* mustard
Serbisches Reisfleisch *zairbishess rīss-flīsh* diced pork, onions, tomatoes and rice
Soleier *zohlī-er* pickled eggs
Soße *zohssuh* sauce, gravy
Spanferkel *shpahnfairkel* sucking pig
Spargel *shpargel* asparagus
Spätzle *shpets-luh* home-made noodles
Speck *shpeck* bacon
Spiegeleier *shpeegelī-er* fried eggs
Spießbraten *shpeess-brahten* joint roasted on a spit
Spinat *shpinaht* spinach
Spitzkohl *shpitskohl* white cabbage
Stachelbeeren *shtaKelbayren* gooseberries
Stollen *shtollen* type of fruit loaf
Streuselkuchen *shtroyzel-kooKen* sponge cake with crumble topping
Sülze *sewltsuh* brawn
Suppen *zoopen* soups
Süßspeisen *sewss-shpīzen* sweet dishes
Szegediner Gulasch *saygaydeener goolash* goulash with pickled cabbage

Törtchen *turtshen* tart(s)
Torte *tortuh* gateau
Thunfisch *toonfish* tuna
Tomatensuppe *tohmahten-zoopuh* tomato soup
Truthahn *troot-hahn* turkey

Überbacken *ewberbacken* coated (with cheese) and grilled
Ungarischer Gulasch *oongarisher goolash* Hungarian goulash

Verlorene Eier *fairlohrenuh ī-er* poached eggs

Vollkornbrot *folkorn-broht* dark rye bread
Vorspeisen *fohrshpīzen* hors d'oeuvres, starters

Waldorfsalat *valdorf-zalaht* salad with celery, apples and walnuts
Weinbergschnecken *vīnbairk-shnecken* snails
Weintrauben *wīntrowben* grapes
Weißbrot *vīss-broht* white bread
Weißkohl *vīss-kohl* white cabbage
Weißwurst *vīss-voorst* veal sausage
Wiener Schnitzel *veener shnitsel* veal in breadcrumbs
Wild *vilt* game
Windbeutel *vint-boytel* cream puff
Wirsing *veerzing* savoy cabbage
Wurst *voorst* sausage
Würstchen *vewrst-shen* frankfurter(s)
Würzig *vewrtsik* spicy

Zigeunerschnitzel *tsigoyner-shnitsel* veal with peppers and relishes
Zitrone *tsitrohnuh* lemon
Zucker *tsoocker* sugar
Zunge *tsoong-uh* tongue
Zwiebeln *tsveebeln* onions
Zwischengerichte *tsvishen-gerishtuh* entrées

MONEY

(*see also BANKS*)

How much is it?
Wieviel kostet es?
veefeel kostet ess

How much is this?
Wieviel kostet das hier?
veefeel kostet dass heer

What does that come to?
Was macht das?
vass mahKt dass

Could you write that down?
Könnten Sie das aufschreiben?
kurnten zee dass owf-shrīben

RESPONSES

Neun Mark achtzig bitte.
noyn mark ahKtsik bittuh
Nine marks eighty please.

Das macht zusammen zwanzig Mark.
dass mahKt tsOOzammen tsvantsik mark
That comes to twenty marks altogether.

Can I use this? (credit card)
Kann ich hiermit bezahlen?
kan ish heermit betsahlen

Can I have the bill please?
Kann ich bitte die Rechnung haben?
kan ish bittuh dee reshnoong hahben

No, I'll pay.
Nein, ich bezahle.
nīn ish betsahluh

Can we pay together/separately?
Können wir zusammen/getrennt bezahlen?
kurnen veer tsoozammen/getrent betsahlen

Can I pay straight away?
Kann ich sofort bezahlen?
kan ish zofort betsahlen

Keep the change.
Der Rest ist für Sie.
dair rest ist fewr zee

Call it 50.
Sagen wir 50.
zahgen veer fewnfzik

That's not right surely.
Das kann nicht stimmen.
dass kan nisht shimmen

That's too expensive.
Das ist zu teuer.
dass ist tsoo toyer

Can you give me coins for this?
Können Sie mir hierfür Münzen geben?
kurnren zee meer heerfewr mewntsen gayben

I'm broke.
Ich bin pleite.
ish bin plītuh

He's loaded.
Er ist steinreich.
air ist shtīnrīsh

Can I have a refund?
Kann ich eine Vergütung haben?
kan ish īnuh fairgewtoong hahben

MONTHS

January	Januar	*yanooar*
February	Februar	*faybrooar*
March	März	*mairts*
April	April	*apreel*
May	Mai	*mī*
June	Juni	*yOOnee*
July	Juli	*yOOlee*
August	August	*owgoost*
September	September	*zeptember*
October	Oktober	*oktohber*
November	November	*november*
December	Dezember	*daytsember*

This month.
Diesen Monat.
deezen mohnaht

Next month/last month.
Nächsten Monat/letzten Monat.
nexsten mohnaht/letsten mohnaht

In March/August.
Im März/August.
im mairts/owgoost

In the summer months.
In den Sommermonaten.
in dayn zommer-mohnahten

During the winter months.
Während der Wintermonate.
vayrent dair vinter-mohnahtuh

NECESSITY, OBLIGATION

Do I have to ...?
Muß ich ...?
mooss ish

We have to go now.
Wir müssen jetzt gehen.
veer mewssen yetst gayen

Is it necessary to pay in advance?
Muß man im voraus bezahlen?
mooss man im forowss betsahlen

That's not necessary.
Das ist nicht nötig.
dass ist nisht nurtik

When do we have to be back by?
Wann müssen wir wieder zurück sein?
van mewssen veer veeder tsOOrewk zīn

You must ...
Sie müssen/du mußt ...
zee mewssen/dOO moost

You must not ...
Sie dürfen/du darfst nicht ...
zee dewrfen/dOO darfst nisht

It must be ready tomorrow.
Es muß bis morgen fertig sein.
ess mooss biss morgen fairtik zīn

You shouldn't do that.
Sie sollten/du solltest das nicht machen.
zee zolten/dOO zoltest dass nisht mahKen

NEGATIVES

To express a negative in German, to say 'I DON'T know', 'it's NOT here' etc, you use the word **nicht**:

Ich weiß. *ish vīss* I know.	**Ich weiß nicht.** *ish vīss nisht* I don't know.
Er hat es. *air hat ess* He's got it.	**Er hat es nicht.** *air hat ess nisht* He hasn't got it.
Sie ist hier. *zee ist heer* She's here.	**Sie ist nicht hier.** *zee ist nisht heer* She's not here.

Note the position of **nicht** in the following sentences:

Bitte seien Sie mir nicht böse.
bittuh zī-en zee meer nisht burzuh
Please don't be angry with me.

Hast du sie nicht gesehen?.
hast doo zee nisht gezayen
Didn't you see her?

Nicht is also used with pronouns:

Ich nicht!
ish nisht
Not me!

To say 'no' with nouns or to say 'not any', use **kein(e)**:

Ich habe kein Geld.
ish hahbuh kīn gelt
I have no money.

Hier gibt es keine Touristen.
heer geept ess kīnuh tooristen
There aren't any tourists here.

NUMBERS

0	null *nool*
1	eins *īnss*
2	zwei *tsvī*
3	drei *drī*
4	vier *feer*
5	fünf *fewnf*
6	sechs *zeks*
7	sieben *zeeben*
8	acht *ahKt*
9	neun *noyn*
10	zehn *tsayn*
11	elf *elf*
12	zwölf *tsvurlf*
13	dreizehn *drī-tsayn*
14	vierzehn *feer-tsayn*
15	fünfzehn *fewnf-tsayn*
16	sechzehn *zesh-tsayn*
17	siebzehn *zeep-tsayn*
18	achtzehn *ahKt-tsayn*
19	neunzehn *noyn-tsayn*
20	zwanzig *tsvantsik*
21	einundzwanzig *īn-oont-tsvantsik*
22	zweiundzwanzig *tsvī-oont-tsvantsik*
30	dreißig *drīssik*
40	vierzig *feertsik*
50	fünfzig *fewnftsik*
60	sechzig *zeshtsik*
70	siebzig *zeeptsik*
80	achtzig *ahKtsik*
90	neunzig *noyntsik*
100	(ein)hundert *(īn)hoondert*
200	zweihundert *tsvīhoondert*
1000	(ein)tausend *(īn)towzent*

87 plus 36.
87 plus 36.
*zeeben-oont-**ah**ĸt**sik** plooss zeks-oont-**drī**ssik*

800 minus 132.
800 minus 132.
*ahĸt-**hoon**dert mee**nooss** īn-hoondert-tsvī-oont-**drī**ssik*

22 times 15.
22 mal 15.
*tsvī-oont-**tsvan**tsik mal **fewnf**-tsayn*

134 divided by 3.
134 geteilt durch 3.
*hoondert-feer-oont-**drī**ssik ge**tīlt** doorsh **drī***

Fourteen and a half.
Vierzehneinhalb.
*feer-tsayn-īn-**halp***

Twelve and a quarter.
Zwölfeinviertel.
*tsvurlf-īn-**feer**tel*

Twelve and three quarters.
Zwölfdreiviertel.
*tsvurlf-drī-**feer**tel*

35 point five, 35.5.
35 Komma fünf, 35,5.
*fewnf-oont-**drī**ssik **kom**ma **fewnf***

10%
Zehn Prozent.
*tsayn prot**sent***

Half as much.
Halb soviel.
*halp zo**feel***

Three times as much.
Dreimal soviel.
drīmal zofeel

How many?
Wie viele?
vee feeluh

How much?
Wieviel?
veefeel

More than 500.
Mehr als 500.
mair alss fewnf-hoondert

Less than 500.
Weniger als 500.
vayniger alss fewnf-hoondert

OFFERING

Can I help?
Kann ich Ihnen behilflich sein?
kan ish eenen behilflish zīn

May I . . .?
Darf ich . . .?
darf ish

Let me do that!
Lassen Sie mich das machen!
lassen zee mish dass mahKen

I'll do that for you.
Ich mache das für Sie.
ish mahKuh dass fewr zee

It's no problem.
Das ist kein Problem.
dass ist kīn problaym

Would you like one?
Möchten Sie einen/eine/eins?
murshten zee īnen/īnuh/īnss

Please take one.
Bitte nehmen Sie einen/eine/eins.
bittuh naymen zee īnen/īnuh/īnss

Please, go on.
Bitte sehr.
bittuh zair

Take mine.
Nehmen Sie meinen/meine/meins.
naymen zee mīnen/mīnuh/mīnss

PAST TENSE

The German imperfect tense refers to a single action in the past or to a length of time in the past. It is used for reporting events that took place in the past and for telling stories:

> **Letztes Jahr waren wir in Spanien.**
> *letstess yar varen veer in shpahnee-en*
> Last year we were in Spain.

> **Dann sagte er mir, daß . . .**
> *dann zahktuh air meer dass*
> Then he told me that . . .

To form the imperfect tense take the **-en** ending off the verb as given in the dictionary section and add the following endings:

ich sag-te	I said
du sag-test (*fam*)	you said
Sie sag-ten (*pol*)	you said
er/sie/es sag-te	he/she/it said
wir sag-ten	we said
ihr sag-tet (*fam*)	you said
Sie sag-ten (*pol*)	you said
sie sag-ten	they said

However there are some verbs, including a number of very common ones, that follow a slightly different pattern. Firstly there is a vowel change in the verb. This is shown in column 3 of the table on page 91. Then these endings are added:

ich sprach	I spoke
du sprach-st (*fam*)	you spoke
Sie sprach-en (*pol*)	you spoke
er/sie/es sprach	he/she/it spoke
wir sprach-en	we spoke
ihr sprach-t (*fam*)	you spoke
Sie sprach-en (*pol*)	you spoke
sie sprach-en	they spoke

A more common way of referring to the past, especially in conversation, is to use the perfect tense. This is formed by combining the present tense of **haben** (to have) or **sein** (to be) with the past participle of the verb. Verbs which form the past tense with **sein** are marked with an asterisk in the dictionary.

The present tense of **haben** and **sein** is as follows:

haben		**sein**	
ich habe	I have	**ich bin**	I am
du hast (*fam*)	you have	**du bist** (*fam*)	you are
Sie haben (*pol*)	you have	**Sie sind** (*pol*)	you are
er/sie/es hat	he/she/it has	**er/sie/es ist**	he/she/it is
wir haben	we have	**wir sind**	we are
ihr habt (*fam*)	you have	**ihr seid** (*fam*)	you are
Sie haben (*pol*)	you have	**Sie sind** (*pol*)	you are
sie haben	they have	**sie sind**	they are

The past participle of a verb ('gone', 'spoken', 'understood' etc in English) is formed by removing the **-en** from the German verb as given in the dictionary section and adding **-t**. For example:

sag-en to say	**gesag-t** said	**ich habe gesagt** I (have) said

Some verbs, as shown in column 4 on page 91, have different endings:

gehen to go	**gegangen** gone	**er ist gegangen** he has gone, he went

I arrived here yesterday.
Ich bin gestern hier angekommen.
ish bin gestern heer angekommen

I didn't see it.
Ich habe es nicht gesehen.
ish hahbuh ess nisht gezayen

Here is a list of the most common German verbs which have special forms in certain tenses. Column 2 is the third person singular of the present tense (he/she stays etc); column 3 is the third person singular of the imperfect tense (he/she stayed etc); column 4 is the past participle (stayed etc).

beginnen *(begin)*	**beginnt**	**begann**	**begonnen**
biegen *(bend)*	**biegt**	**bog**	**gebogen**
bleiben* *(stay)*	**bleibt**	**blieb**	**geblieben**
bringen *(bring)*	**bringt**	**brachte**	**gebracht**
dürfen *(be allowed to)*	**darf**	**durfte**	**gedurft**
essen *(eat)*	**ißt**	**aß**	**gegessen**
fahren* *(drive, go)*	**fährt**	**fuhr**	**gefahren**
finden *(find)*	**findet**	**fand**	**gefunden**
fliegen* *(fly)*	**fliegt**	**flog**	**geflogen**
geben *(give)*	**gibt**	**gab**	**gegeben**
gehen* *(go)*	**geht**	**ging**	**gegangen**
haben *(have)*	**hat**	**hatte**	**gehabt**
kennen *(know)*	**kennt**	**kannte**	**gekannt**
kommen* *(come)*	**kommt**	**kam**	**gekommen**
können *(be able to)*	**kann**	**konnte**	**gekonnt**
lassen *(let, allow)*	**läßt**	**ließ**	**gelassen**
lesen *(read)*	**liest**	**las**	**gelesen**
liegen *(lie)*	**liegt**	**lag**	**gelegen**
müssen *(have to)*	**muß**	**mußte**	**gemußt**
nehmen *(take)*	**nimmt**	**nahm**	**genommen**
schließen *(shut)*	**schließt**	**schloß**	**geschlossen**
schreiben *(write)*	**schreibt**	**schrieb**	**geschrieben**
schwimmen* *(swim)*	**schwimmt**	**schwamm**	**geschwommen**
sehen *(see)*	**sieht**	**sah**	**gesehen**
sein* *(be)*	**ist**	**war**	**gewesen**
sitzen *(sit)*	**sitzt**	**saß**	**gesessen**
steigen* *(climb)*	**steigt**	**stieg**	**gestiegen**
sterben* *(die)*	**stirbt**	**starb**	**gestorben**
trinken *(drink)*	**trinkt**	**trank**	**getrunken**
tun *(do)*	**tut**	**tat**	**getan**
verlieren *(lose)*	**verliert**	**verlor**	**verloren**
werden* *(become)*	**wird**	**wurde**	**geworden**
wissen *(know)*	**weiß**	**wußte**	**gewußt**
wollen *(want to)*	**will**	**wollte**	**gewollt**

PERMISSION

Can I . . .?
Kann ich . . . ?
kan ish

Can we . . .?
Können wir . . . ?
kurnen veer

Can he/she . . .?
Kann er/sie . . . ?
kan air/zee

Can they . . .?
Können sie . . . ?
kurnen zee

Can I go in?
Kann ich hineingehen?
kan ish hinīngayen

Is it allowed?
Ist es erlaubt?
ist ess airlowpt

Is that all right?
Ist das in Ordnung?
ist dass in ortnoong

Can you give me a permit?
Können Sie mir eine Genehmigung geben?
kurnen zee meer īnuh genaymigoong gayben

Yes that's ok, on you go.
Ja natürlich.
ya natewrlish

PHOTOGRAPHS

Do you have a film for this camera?
Haben Sie einen Film für diese Kamera?
hahben zee īnen film fewr deezuh kamera

35/16mm.
35/16 Millimeter.
fewnf-oont-drīssik/zesh-tsayn milimayter

12/24/36 exposures.
12/24/36 Bilder.
tsvurlf/feer-oont-tsvantsik/zeks-oont-drīssik bilder

Can you develop these?
Können Sie diese entwickeln?
kurnen zee deezuh entvickeln

I'd like prints/slides.
Ich hätte gerne Abzüge/Dias.
ish hettuh gairnuh ap-tsewguh/dee-ahs

Can you make another print of these two?
Können Sie von diesen beiden noch einen Abzug machen?
kurnen zee fon deezen bīden noK īnen aptsOOk mahKen

Excuse me, could you take a photograph of me/us?
Entschuldigung, könnten Sie von mir/uns ein Foto machen?
entshooldigoong kurnten zee fon meer/oonss īn fohto mahKen

Smile!
Bitte lächeln!
bittuh lesheln

Filmentwicklung.
filmentvickloong
Film processing.

PLURALS

Many German nouns form their plural simply by adding **-e**:

der Freund	**die Freunde**	friend(s)
das Bein	**die Beine**	leg(s)

Another way of forming the plural is by adding **-n** or **-en**:

der Staat	**die Staaten**	state(s)
die Stunde	**die Stunden**	hour(s)
das Bett	**die Betten**	bed(s)

Some masculine and neuter nouns do not change at all:

der Kuchen	**die Kuchen**	cake(s)
das Messer	**die Messer**	knife (knives)

Many nouns containing an **a**, **o** or **u** add an umlaut (*see PRONUNCIATION*) in the plural and use either no ending or add **-e** or **-er**:

der Mann	**die Männer**	man (men)
der Apfel	**die Äpfel**	apple(s)
die Hand	**die Hände**	hand(s)
die Mutter	**die Mütter**	mother(s)
das Buch	**die Bücher**	book(s)

Some nouns, especially ones of foreign origin, add **-s** to form the plural:

der Punk	**die Punks**	punk(s)
die Disco	**die Discos**	disco(s)
das Hotel	**die Hotels**	hotel(s)
das Auto	**die Autos**	car(s)

There are few general rules concerning the formation of plurals, and it is advisable to learn each plural along with the noun concerned. The following list of noun endings may, however, be helpful:

noun ending	*gender*	*plural*
-ar	*m*	**-are**
-är	*m*	**-äre**
-chen	*n*	**-chen**
-e	*m,f,n*	**-en**
-eur	*m*	**-eure**
-ich	*m*	**-iche**
-heit	*f*	**-heiten**
-in	*f*	**-innen**
-ium	*n*	**-ien**
-keit	*f*	**-keiten**
-lein	*n*	**-lein**
-ling	*m*	**-linge**
-nis	*n*	**-nisse**
-or	*m*	**-oren**
-schaft	*f*	**-schaften**
-ung	*f*	**-ungen**

POLICE AND THE LAW

(*see also* *CAR ACCIDENTS, THEFT*)

Could you come with me, there's been some trouble.
Kommen Sie bitte, es hat Ärger gegeben.
kommen zee bittuh ess hat airger gegayben

He started it.
Er hat angefangen.
air hat an-gefangen

It wasn't my fault.
Es war nicht meine Schuld.
ess var nisht mīnuh shoolt

It was his/her fault.
Es war seine/ihre Schuld.
ess var zīnuh/eeruh shoolt

RESPONSES

Ihr Name, bitte?
eer nahmuh bittuh
Your name please?

Ihre Adresse?
eeruh adressuh
Your address?

Kann ich Ihren Paß sehen?
kan ish eeren pas zayen
Can I see your passport?

Ausweis bitte.
owss-vīss bittuh
Papers please.

I didn't know it wasn't allowed.
Ich wußte nicht, daß es verboten war.
ish voostuh nisht dass ess fairbohten var

There's no sign up.
Da ist kein Schild.
da ist kīn shilt

It's not mine, I rented it.
Es gehört mir nicht, ich habe es gemietet.
ess gehurt meer nisht ish hahbuh ess gemeetet

I want to report a loss.
Ich möchte eine Verlustmeldung machen.
ish murshtuh īnuh fairloost-meldoong mahKen

. . . has gone missing.
. . . ist verschwunden.
. . . ist fairshvoonden

He/she was wearing . . .
Er/sie trug . . .
air/zee trOOk

He/she has blue/brown eyes.
Er/sie hat blaue/braune Augen.
air/zee hat blowuh/brownuh owgen

He/she has blonde/red hair.
Er/sie hat blonde/rote Haare.
air/zee hat blonduh/rohtuh haruh

POSSESSIVES

The possessive adjectives ('my', 'your' etc) are:

	m	*f*	*n*	*pl*
my	**mein**	**meine**	**mein**	**meine**
your (*fam*)	**dein**	**deine**	**dein**	**deine**
(*pol*)	**Ihr**	**Ihre**	**Ihr**	**Ihre**
his	**sein**	**seine**	**sein**	**seine**
her	**ihr**	**ihre**	**ihr**	**ihre**
our	**unser**	**unsere**	**unser**	**unsere**
your (*fam*)	**euer**	**eure**	**euer**	**eure**
(*pol*)	**Ihr**	**Ihre**	**Ihr**	**Ihre**
their	**ihr**	**ihre**	**ihr**	**ihre**

That's my room.
Das ist mein Zimmer.
dass ist mīn tsimmer

We'll meet at your hotel.
Wir treffen uns in Ihrem Hotel.
veer treffen oonss in eerem hohtel

When another adjective is used with these words it takes the same endings as adjectives following **ein** (*see ADJECTIVES*):

Her old car.
Ihr altes Auto.
eer altess owto

My new shoes.
Meine neuen Schuhe.
mīnuh noy-en shOO-uh

Possessive pronouns ('mine', 'yours' etc) are formed by adding **-er** to the masculine and **-(e)s** to the neuter forms of the possessive adjectives. The feminine and plural forms are the same as the possessive adjectives:

Dieser Mantel? Das ist meiner.
deezer mantel dass ist mīner
That coat? It's mine.

Ist das Glas Ihres oder seins?
ist das glahss eeress ohder zīnss
Is that glass yours or his?

POSSIBILITIES

Is it possible to . . .?
Ist es möglich zu . . . ?
ist ess murglish tsoo

Could I possibly borrow this?
Könnte ich dies möglicherweise ausleihen?
kurntuh ish deess murglisher-vīzuh owss-lī-en

I might, I'm not sure.
Vielleicht, ich bin nicht sicher.
feelīsht ish bin nisht zisher

We might want to stay longer.
Wir möchten vielleicht länger bleiben.
veer murshten feelīsht leng-er blīben

He might have.
Vielleicht.
feelīsht

They might have left already.
Sie sind vielleicht schon abgefahren.
zee zint feelīsht shohn ap-gefaren

Who knows?
Wer weiß?
vair vīss

There's an outside chance.
Es besteht eine geringe Chance.
ess beshtayt īnuh gering-uh shonssuh

That's out of the question!
Das kommt nicht in Frage!
dass kommt nisht in frahghuh

POST OFFICE

Two stamps for letters to the UK please.
Zweimal Briefporto nach Großbritannien, bitte.
tsvīmal breefporto nahK grohss-britahnee-en bittuh

Eight stamps for postcards to England please.
Acht Briefmarken für Postkarten nach England, bitte.
ahKt breefmarken fewr posstkarten nahK eng-lant bittuh

Do you have three airmail letters?
Haben Sie drei Luftpostbriefe?
hahben zee drī looftposst-breefuh

I'd like to send this registered.
Ich möchte dies gerne per Einschreiben schicken.
ish murshtuh deess gairnuh pair īnshrīben shicken

Is there any mail for me?
Ist Post für mich da?
ist posst fewr mish da

YOU'LL SEE

Postwertzeichen in kleinen Mengen.
posstvairtsīchen in klīnen meng-en
Stamps (small quantities).

Postlagernde Sendungen.
posst-lahgernduh zendoong-en
Poste restante.

Ausland.
owsslant
Overseas.

Nächste Leerung.
nexstuh layroong
Next collection.

PRACTISING YOUR GERMAN

Here are twenty questions about German. All of them can be answered by using the information given in the various sections of this book. The answers are on the next page.

1. What is the German for 'we are'?
2. What is the plural of **der Junge/die Zeitung/das Buch**?
3. What is the German for 'we can'?
4. **Ich bin müde** means 'I am tired'. What is 'I am not tired'?
5. Which case do you use after **mit** (German for 'with')?
6. How do you say 'with a hammer'?
7. **Sie** is the polite pronoun for 'you'. What is the familiar pronoun?
8. **Leicht** means 'easy'. How do you say 'easier'?
9. How do you say 'faster than his car'?
10. What is the German for 'on Tuesdays'?
11. What do the signs **Gleis/Auskunft** mean?
12. If you order a **Sekt** to drink what will you get?
13. How would you ask for a single room for two nights?
14. How do you ask for the bill in a restaurant?
15. What is **Rindfleisch**?
16. **Ich bin sehr froh** means 'I'm very pleased. Say 'I was very pleased'.
17. How do you say 'I come from . . .'?
18. How do you ask someone their name?
19. If someone says 'thanks very much' to you in German what could you reply?
20. How do you pronounce **Bein/braun/viel**?

PRACTISING YOUR GERMAN – ANSWERS

1. Wir sind.
2. Die Jungen, die Zeitungen, die Bücher.
3. Wir können.
4. Ich bin nicht müde.
5. The dative.
6. Mit einem Hammer.
7. Du.
8. Leichter.
9. Schneller als sein Auto.
10. Dienstags.
11. Platform/Information.
12. Sparkling wine.
13. Ich hätte gerne ein Einzelzimmer für zwei Nächte.
14. Ich hätte gern die Rechnung.
15. Beef.
16. Ich war sehr froh.
17. Ich komme aus . . .
18. Wie heißen Sie/wie heißt du?
19. Bitte schön.
20. *bīn/brown/feel*

PRESENT TENSE

To say something in the present tense – for example 'I am going' or 'do you speak?' – you need to know the present tense endings. These are as follows:

gehen	*(to go)*	**sprechen** (to speak)
I	**ich geh-e**	**ich sprech-e**
you *(fam)*	**du geh-st**	**du sprich-st**
you *(pol)*	**Sie geh-en**	**Sie sprech-en**
he/she/it	**er/sie/es geh-t**	**er/sie/es sprich-t**
we	**wir geh-en**	**wir sprech-en**
you *(fam pl)*	**ihr geh-t**	**ihr sprech-t**
you *(pol pl)*	**Sie geh-en**	**Sie sprech-en**
they	**sie geh-en**	**sie sprech-en**

Note that in German you can also sometimes use the present tense when in English you would use the future tense (*see FUTURE*):

Ich nehme diese.
ish naymuh deezuh
I'll take these.

Sometimes German uses the present where English uses the past:

Wir sind seit zwei Wochen hier.
veer zint zīt tsvī voKen heer
We've been here for two weeks.

Here is the present tense of some useful verbs which differ from the rules given in the table above:

dürfen (to be allowed to)

ich darf *(I may)*	**wir dürfen**
du darfst	**ihr dürft**
Sie dürfen	**Sie dürfen**
er/sie/es darf	**sie dürfen**

können (to be able to)

ich kann (*I can*)	**wir können**
du kannst	**ihr könnt**
Sie können	**Sie können**
er/sie/es kann	**sie können**

müssen (to have to)

ich muß (*I must*)	**wir müssen**
du mußt	**ihr müßt**
Sie müssen	**Sie müssen**
er/sie/es muß	**sie müssen**

wissen (to know)

ich weiß	**wir wissen**
du weißt	**ihr wißt**
Sie wissen	**Sie wissen**
er/sie/es weiß	**sie wissen**

wollen (to want (to))

ich will	**wir wollen**
du willst	**ihr wollt**
Sie wollen	**Sie wollen**
er/sie/es will	**sie wollen**

PRONOUNS

If you are using a pronoun as the subject of a verb, saying 'HE is' or 'WE are' etc, the words are:

ich	*ish*	I	**wir**	*veer*	we
du	*doo*	you	**ihr**	*eer*	you
Sie	*zee*	you	**Sie**	*zee*	you
er	*air*	he/it	**sie**	*zee*	they
sie	*zee*	she/it			
es	*ess*	it			

Points to note:

YOU: **du** (*singular*) and **ihr** (*plural*) are used when speaking to someone who is a friend, or to people of your own general age group with whom you want to establish a friendly atmosphere. **Sie** (*singular and plural*) is used when speaking to people you don't know as friends. In the vast majority of cases when travelling as a foreigner in Germany you will use the **Sie** form. Certainly, if you are in any doubt as to which form to use, choose the **Sie** form.

IT: if you are using 'it' to refer to something like 'the train', 'the tram', 'the car' etc (as opposed to saying 'it is cold today' etc) you should use **er**, **sie** or **es** depending on the gender of the thing you are talking about (*see ARTICLES*). For example, **der Zug** (*the train*) is **er** (*it*), **die Straßenbahn** (*the tram*) is **sie** (*it*) and **das Auto** (*the car*) is **es** (*it*).

If you are using the pronoun as an object, saying 'I know HIM' or 'he saw THEM' etc, use the following words:

mich	*mish*	me	**uns**	*oonss*	us
dich	*dish*	you	**euch**	*oysh*	you
Sie	*zee*	you	**Sie**	*zee*	you
ihn	*een*	him/it	**sie**	*zee*	them
sie	*zee*	her/it			
es	*ess*	it			

I know him.
Ich kenne ihn.
ish kennuh een

He saw them.
Ich habe sie gesehen.
ish hahbuh zee gezayen

Do you understand me?
Verstehen Sie mich?
fershtayen zee mish

Note: **Who's that? – It's me.**
Wer ist das? – Ich bin's.
vair ist das – ish binss

If you are using a pronoun to say, for example, you sent something TO HER or that you spoke TO HIM, then use the following words:

mir	*meer*	to me	**uns**	*oonss*	to us
dir	*deer*	to you	**euch**	*oysh*	to you
Ihnen	*eenen*	to you	**Ihnen**	*eenen*	to you
ihm	*eem*	to him/it	**ihnen**	*eenen*	to them
ihr	*eer*	to her/it			

I gave it to him.
Ich habe es ihm gegeben.
ish hahbuh ess eem gegayben

She sent me a letter.
Sie hat mir einen Brief geschickt.
zee hat meer īnen breef geshickt

Note that most German prepositions (words like FOR, WITH, AFTER, ON, UNDER etc) take either the accusative or the dative, ie 'me' would either be **mich** or **mir**, 'him' would either be **ihn** or **ihm** etc. (*See also CASES*).

Some examples:

This is for you.
Das ist für dich/Sie.
dass ist fewr dish/zee

After him/us.
Nach ihm/uns.
nahk eem/oonss

PRONUNCIATION

As compared with English, German is a very regular language when it comes to pronunciation. The following general guidelines to special sounds in German will help you pronounce new German words that you encounter. To get the actual values of the sounds listen carefully to a German speaker and try to copy what you hear. (*See also the INTRODUCTION*).

ä	either as in day (spät, Träne) or as in men (Männer, ändern)
ö	as in fur (Köln, Mörder)
ü/y	prepare your mouth to say oo, then make an ee sound (führen, München)
au	as in cow (Augsburg, braun)
äu	as in joy (träumen)
ee	as in day (Beethoven)
ei	as in shy (klein, Heidelberg)
eu	as in joy (Deutschland)
ie	as in seen (die, nieder)
oo	as in bone (Boot)
b	when in final position like a p (ab)
ch	like Scottish loch after a, au, o and u; otherwise nearer to sh
d	when in final position like a t (Sand)
g	when in final position like a k (Tag)
j	as in yes (ja, jetzt)
qu	pronounced kv (Quittung)
s	like a z (Saarland, Insel)
sch	pronounced sh (Schule)
sp/st	at the beginning of a word or syllable pronounced shp/sht (Sport, Stuttgart,aufstehen)
ß	pronounced ss (muß)
th	pronounced t (Theater)
v	pronounced f (von)
w	pronounced v (Wiesbaden)
z	pronounced ts (Zug, Zimmer)

QUESTIONS

What is . . .?
Was ist . . . ?
vass ist

Where is . . .?
Wo ist . . . ?
voh ist

When is . . .?
Wann ist . . . ?
van ist

Which is . . .?
Welcher/welche/welches ist . . . ?
velsher/velshuh/velshess ist

Who is . . .?
Wer ist . . . ?
vair ist

Why is . . .?
Warum ist . . . ?
varoom ist

How long will it take?
Wie lange dauert es?
vee lang-uh dowert ess

How do I get to . . .?
Wie komme ich nach . . . ?
vee kommuh ish nahK

How do you do it?
Wie macht man das?
vee mahKt man dass

What are these?
Was sind das?
vass zint dass

Where are we going?
Wohin gehen wir?
vohin gayen veer

Which are mine?
Welche sind meine?
velshuh zint mīnuh

Can you tell me . . .?
Können Sie mir sagen . . . ?
kurnen zee meer zahgen

Can you . . .?
Können Sie/kannst du . . . ?
kurnen zee/kanst doo

Can I . . .?
Kann ich . . . ?
kan ish

Can we . . .?
Können wir . . . ?
kurnen veer

Can he/she . . .?
Kann er/sie . . . ?
kan air/zee

Could you write it down?
Könnten Sie es aufschreiben?
kurnten zee ess owf-shrīben

REFERRING TO THINGS/PEOPLE

This one.
Dieser/diese/dieses hier.
deezer/deezuh/deezess heer

That one.
Der/die/das da.
dair/dee/dass da

Not that one, the one behind it.
Nicht der/die/das, der/die/das dahinter.
nisht dair/dee/dass dair/dee/dass dahinter

That one over there.
Der/die/das da drüben.
dair/dee/dass da drewben

The man over there.
Der Mann da drüben.
dair man da drewben

Him/her.
Er/sie.
air/zee

Him in the green shirt.
Der mit dem grünen Hemd.
dair mit daym grewnen hemt

The woman next to her.
Die Frau neben ihr.
dee frow nayben eer

These two/those two.
Diese zwei/die zwei da.
deezuh tsvī/dee tsvī da

No, no, the other one.
Nein, nein, der/die/das andere.
nīn nīn dair/dee/dass anderuh

RENTALS

I want to hire a car/bike.
Ich möchte ein Auto/Fahrrad mieten.
ish murshtuh īn owto/faraht meeten

Can I rent one for a day/two days/a week?
Kann ich eins für einen Tag/zwei Tage/eine Woche mieten?
kan ish īnss fewr īnen tahk/tsvī tahguh/īnuh voKuh meeten

How much is it per day?
Wieviel kostet es pro Tag?
veefeel kostet ess pro tahk

When do we have to bring it back?
Wann müssen wir es zurückbringen?
van mewssen veer ess tsOOrewk-bring-en

RESPONSES

Ihren Führerschein/Paß, bitte.
eeren fewrer-shīn/pas bittuh
Your licence/passport please.

Wo wohnen Sie?
vo vohnen zee
Where are you staying?

I'm at Hotel . . .
Ich wohne im Hotel . . .
ish vohnuh im hohtel

It's rented.
Es ist gemietet.
ess ist gemeetet

REPAIRS

(*see also GARAGES*)

Can you fix this?
Können Sie dies reparieren?
kurnen zee deess repareeren

It's broken.
Es ist kaputt.
ess ist kapoot

Can you put new soles on these?
Können Sie diese neu besohlen?
kurnen zee deezuh noy bezohlen

Can you re-heel these?
Können Sie neue Absätze anbringen?
kurnen zee noyuh ap-zetsuh an-bring-en

Can you put a patch on this?
Können Sie hier einen Flicken aufsetzen?
kurnen zee heer īnen flicken owf-zetsen

Can you replace this?
Können Sie dies ersetzen?
kurnen zee deess airzetsen

It needs a new . . .
Es braucht einen neuen/eine neue/ein neues . . .
ess browKt īnen noyen/īnuh noyuh/īn noyess

Can you do it today/by tomorrow?
Können Sie es heute noch/bis morgen machen?
kurnen zee ess hoytuh noK/biss morgen mahKen

Can you write the price down?
Können Sie den Preis aufschreiben?
kurnen zee dayn prīss owf-shrīben

REQUESTS

Could you please . . .?
Könnten Sie bitte . . .?
kurnten zee bittuh

Could you tell me . . .?
Könnten Sie mir bitte sagen . . .?
kurnten zee meer bittuh zahgen

Could you give this to her?
Könnten Sie ihr dies geben?
kurnten zee eer deess gayben

Could I . . .?
Könnte ich . . .?
kurntuh ish

Could I have . . .?
Könnte ich . . . haben?
kurntuh ish . . . hahben

Could we have another?
Könnten wir noch einen/eine/eins haben?
kurnten veer noK īnen/īnuh/īnss hahben

Please leave it open.
Bitte lassen Sie es offen.
bittuh lassen zee ess offen

Please don't.
Bitte nicht.
bittuh nisht

Please don't speak so fast.
Bitte sprechen Sie nicht so schnell.
bittuh shpreshen zee nisht zo shnel

RESTAURANTS

(*see also MENU READER and DICTIONARY*)

A table for one/two please.
Einen Einzeltisch/einen Tisch für zwei Personen, bitte.
īnen īntseltish/īnen tish fewr tsvī pairzohnen bittuh

Can I book a table for this evening?
Kann ich für heute Abend einen Tisch reservieren?
kan ish fewr hoytuh ahbent īnen tish rezerveeren

I've booked a table.
Ich habe einen Tisch reserviert.
ish hahbuh īnen tish rezerveert

The name is . . .
Der Name ist . . .
dair nahmuh ist

Can I see the menu?
Kann ich die Speisekarte sehen?
kan ish dee shpīzuh-kartuh zayen

Can I see the wine list please?
Kann ich bitte die Weinkarte sehen?
kan ish bittuh dee vīn-kartuh zayen

A litre of house red please.
Einen Liter roten Tafelwein, bitte.
īnen leeter rohten tahfelvīn bittuh

Half a litre of house white please.
Einen halben Liter weißen Tafelwein, bitte.
īnen halben leeter vīssen tahfelvīn bittuh

Waiter!
Herr Ober!
hair ohber

Miss!
Fräulein!
froylīn

That's for me thanks.
Das ist für mich, danke.
dass ist fewr mish dankuh

That's for him/her.
Das ist für ihn/sie.
dass ist fewr een/zee

I didn't order this.
Das habe ich nicht bestellt.
*dass **hah**buh ish nisht beshtellt*

I ordered red wine.
Ich habe Rotwein bestellt.
*ish **hah**buh **roh**tvīn beshtellt*

I'm afraid this tastes funny.
Dies schmeckt leider recht merkwürdig.
*deess shmeckt **lī**der resht **mair**kvewrdik*

Two coffees please.
Zwei Kaffee, bitte.
*tsvī **ka**fay **bi**ttuh*

One cappuccino and one espresso.
Einen Cappuccino und einen Espresso.
īnen kapOOcheeno oont īnen espresso

That was absolutely excellent!
Das war ganz ausgezeichnet!
dass var gants owss-getsīshnet

Best meal of the holiday!
Das beste Essen des Urlaubs!
*dass **be**stuh essen dess OOrlowps*

Can I have the bill please?
Ich hätte gern die Rechnung.
ish hettuh gairn dee reshnoong

ROAD SIGNS

Achtung! Straßenbahn Beware trams!
Anlieger frei residents only
Ausfahrt freihalten keep exit clear
Autobahnraststätte motorway services area
Bitte einordnen get in lane
Einbahnstraße one way street
Einfahrt freilassen keep entrance clear
Erst gurten, dann starten clunk click every trip
Fahrradweg cycle path
Fußgänger bitte andere Straßenseite benutzen pedestrians please use other pavement
use other pavement
Gefährliche Einmündung dangerous junction
Gesperrt für Fahrzeuge aller Art closed to all vehicles
Glatteisgefahr black ice
Kriechspur crawler lane
Langsam fahren drive slowly
Licht einschalten switch lights on
Linksabbieger left filter
LKW lorry, heavy goods vehicle
Motor abstellen switch engine off
Nebel fog
Nicht hupen sounding horn is forbidden
Nur für Anlieger residents only
Pannenhilfe breakdown service
Parken nur mit Parkscheibe parking discs compulsory
Rechtsabbieger right filter
Rollsplit loose chippings
Sackgasse dead end
Schlechte Fahrbahn poor road surface
Seitenstreifen nicht befahrbar soft verges
Straßenarbeiten roadworks
Tankstelle petrol station
Umleitung diversion
Unfallgefahr accident black spot
Vorfahrt beachten give way
Vorsichtig fahren drive with care
Widerrechtlich abgestellte Fahrzeuge werden kostenpflichtig abgeschleppt illegally parked vehicles will be towed away at the owner's expense

ROOMS – FINDING A ROOM

(*see also HOTELS*)

I'm looking for a room.
Ich suche ein Zimmer.
ish zOOKuh īn tsimmer

Where can I find a room that's not too expensive?
Wo kann ich ein Zimmer finden, das nicht zu teuer ist?
vo kan ish īn tsimmer finden dass nisht tsOO toyer ist

What's a good area for finding a room?
In welchem Stadtteil findet man am besten ein Zimmer?
in velshem shtat-tīl findet man am besten īn tsimmer

Just one night/three nights.
Nur eine Nacht/drei Nächte.
nOOr īnuh nahKt/drī neshtuh

Just one person/there are two of us.
Nur eine Person/wir sind zu zweit.
nOOr īnuh pairzohn/veer zint tsOO tsvīt

Could you write the address down for me?
Könnten Sie mir die Adresse aufschreiben?
kurnten zee meer dee adressuh owf-shrīben

Could you ring them from here to check?
Könnten Sie sie von hier aus anrufen und nachfragen?
kurnten zee zee fon heer owss an-rOOfen oont nahK-frahgen

RESPONSES

Die Stadt ist völlig ausgebucht.
dee shtat ist furlik owss-gebOOKt
The town is absolutely full up.

Versuchen Sie . . .
fairzOOKen zee
Try . . .

Could you check the cooker/fridge/shower?
Könnten Sie den Herd/den Kühlschrank/die Dusche überprüfen?
kurnten zee dayn hairt/dayn kewl-shrank/dee dOOshuh ewber-prewfen

How does the ... work?
Wie funktioniert der/die/das ...?
vee foonkts-yohneert dair/dee/dass

The maid wasn't there today.
Die Hausangestellte war heute nicht da.
dee howss-an-geshtelltuh var hoytuh nisht da

The people next door to us make a terrible noise.
Die Leute nebenan machen einen schrecklichen Lärm.
dee loytuh naybenan mahKen īnen shrecklishen lairm

Could you maybe have a quiet word with them?
Könnten Sie vielleicht mal ein Wörtchen mit ihnen reden?
kurnten zee feelīsht mal īn vurtshen mit eenen rayden

When does the shop open/close?
Wann öffnet/schließt das Geschäft?
van urfnet/shleest dass gesheft

Could we have some clean bedding?
Könnten wir sauberes Bettzeug bekommen?
kurnten veer zowberess bet-tsoyg bekommen

Thank you for looking after us.
Danke, daß Sie sich um uns gekümmert haben.
dankuh dass zee zish oom oonss gekewmert hahben

SHOPPING

I've got some shopping to do.
Ich muß einkaufen gehen.
ish moos īnkowfen gayen

He's gone to the shops.
Er ist einkaufen gegangen.
air ist īnkowfen gegang-en

Do you have ...?
Haben Sie ... ?
hahben zee

I'm just looking thanks.
Ich schaue mich nur um, danke.
ish showuh mish nOOr oom dankuh

Can I have a look around?
Kann ich mich etwas umschauen?
kan ish mish etvass oom-showen

How much is this?
Wieviel kostet das hier?
veefeel kostet dass heer

Do you have other colours?
Haben Sie auch andere Farben?
hahben zee owK anderuh farben

Do you have any smaller ones?
Haben Sie auch kleinere?
hahben zee owK klīneruh

Do you have any bigger ones?
Haben Sie auch größere?
hahben zee owK grursseruh

It's not really what I'm looking for.
Es ist nicht das, wonach ich suche.
ess ist nisht dass vonahK ish zOOKuh

That's fine, I'll take it.
Das ist gut, das nehme ich.
dass ist gOOt dass naymuh ish

Could you gift-wrap it for me?
Könnten Sie es für mich als Geschenk einpacken?
kurnten zee ess fewr mish alss geshenk īnpacken

Can I use this? (credit card)
Kann ich hiermit bezahlen?
kan ish heermit betsahlen

YOU'LL SEE

Schlußverkauf.
shloossfairkowf
Sale.

Preissenkung.
prīss-zenkoong
Reduced prices.

SHOP NAMES

Apotheke *apotaykuh* Dispensing chemist
Bäckerei *beckerī* Baker
Buchhandlung *booKhandloong* Bookshop
Drogerie *drohgeree* Chemist
Friseur *freezur* Hairdresser
Kaufhaus *kowfhowss* Department store
Konditorei *konditorī* Cake shop/café
Lebensmittelgeschäft *laybens-mittel-gesheft* Foodstore
Metzgerei *metsgerī* Butcher
Reinigung *rīnigoong* Dry cleaning
Reisebüro *rīzuh-bewro* Travel agency
Schlachterei *shlaKterī* Butcher
Schreibwarengeschäft *shrīp-varen-gesheft* Stationer

SIGHTSEEING

Do you have a map of the area?
Haben Sie eine Karte von diesem Gebiet?
hahben zee īnuh kartuh fon deezem gebeet

Do you have a guidebook for the area?
Haben Sie einen Reiseführer über dieses Gebiet?
hahben zee īnen rīzuh-fewrer ewber deezes gebeet

Are there any guided tours (of the city/the area)?
Gibt es Führungen (in der Stadt/in diesem Gebiet)?
geept ess fewroong-en (in dair shtat/in deezem gebeet)

We want to go to Heidelberg.
Wir möchten nach Heidelberg.
veer murshten nahK hīdelbairk

We want to go to Neuschwanstein.
Wir möchten zum Schloß Neuschwanstein.
veer murshten tsoom shloss noyshvahnshtīn

We've been seeing the sights.
Wir haben die Sehenswürdigkeiten gesehen.
veer hahben dee zayens-vewrdik-kīten gezayen

I want to see the real Hamburg/Deutschland.
Ich möchte das echte Hamburg/Deutschland kennenlernen.
ish murshtuh dass eshtuh hamboork/doytshlant kennenlairnen

Can you give us the name of a really typical restaurant?
Können Sie uns ein wirklich typisches Restaurant nennen?
kurnen zee oonss īn veerklish tewpishess restoron nennen

Stadtrundfahrt.
shtatroontfart
City tour.

SIGNS

Abfahrt departure(s)
Angeln verboten no fishing
Ankunft arrival(s)
Anmeldung reception, registration
Anschluß an ... connecting with ...
Aufzug lift
Aus off, out
Ausgang exit
Auskunft information
Ausländische Währungen foreign currencies
Außer Betrieb out of order
Außer samstags/sonntags except Saturdays/Sundays
Autovermietung car hire
Baden verboten no bathing
Bahnhof station
Bahnsteig platform
Besetzt occupied, engaged
Betreten auf eigene Gefahr enter at own risk
Betreten des Rasens nicht gestattet keep of the grass
Betriebsbereit ready for use
Betteln und Hausieren verboten no beggars, no hawkers
Biologisch abbaubar biodegradable
Bitte klingeln please ring
Bootsverleih boats for hire
Damen ladies
Defekt faulty
Deutsches Erzeugnis made in Germany
Doppelzimmer double room
Drücken push
Durchgang passage
Durchgehend geöffnet open 24 hours/all day
Ein in, on
Eingang entrance
Einlaß admission
Eintritt frei admission free
Eltern haften für ihre Kinder parents are responsible for their children
Erfrischungen refreshments
Erste Hilfe first aid
Erwachsene adults
Etage floor
Fahrkarten tickets

Fahrradweg cycle path
Fahrstuhl lift
Fernsprecher telephone
Feuergefahr fire hazard
Feuertreppe fire escape
Flughafen airport
Flugsteig gate
Frei free, vacant
Frei von Konservierungsstoffen no preservatives
Fremdenzimmer rooms to let
Frisch gestrichen wet paint
Führungen guided tours
Für Jugendliche ab ... Jahren for young people over ...
Fußgängerzone pedestrian precinct
Gebrauchsanweisung beachten follow instructions for use
Gebührenpflichtig subject to a charge
Geld einwerfen insert money
Geldrückgabe coins returned
Geöffnet von ... bis ... open from ... to ...
Gepäckaufbewahrung left luggage
Gepäckausgabe baggage claim
Geschlossen closed
Giftig poisonous
Gleis platform
Grenze border
Haltestelle stop
Hauptbahnhof central station
Herren gents
Hier abreißen/abschneiden tear off/cut off here
Hunde bitte anleinen dogs must be on leash
Im Notfall Scheibe einschlagen smash glass in case of emergency
Jugendherberge youth hostel
Keine heiße Asche einfüllen do not place hot ashes in this container
Kein Einstieg no entrance
Keine Selbstbedienung no self-service
Kein Trinkwasser not drinking water
Kein Zutritt no admission, keep out
Kinder children
Krankenhaus hospital
Lebensgefahr danger

Mindestens haltbar bis ... will keep until at least ...
Mißbrauch strafbar penalty for improper use
Mitfahrzentrale agency which arranges lifts (for a fee)
Mittags geschlossen closed at lunchtime
Nächste Leerung next collection
Nicht berühren do not touch
Nichtraucher non-smoking
Notausgang emergency exit
Notbremse emergency brake
Notruf emergency services
Nur begrenzt haltbar will not keep
Öffnungszeiten opening hours
Plakate ankleben verboten stick no bills
Preise prices
Rauchen verboten no smoking
Raucher smoking
Reiseauskunft travel information
Ruf doch mal an why not make that phonecall?
Ruhetag closing day
Schließfächer luggage lockers
Schutt abladen verboten no dumping
Schwimmbad swimming pool
Sitz für Schwerbehinderte seat for disabled persons
Sonderangebot special offer
Trimm-dich-Pfad jogging path with exercise bars etc
Tür schließen close door
U-Bahn underground
Verboten forbidden
Voll belegt full, no vacancies
Vom Umtausch ausgeschlossen no exchange allowed
Vorsicht Stufe! mind the step
Vorsicht bissiger Hund! beware of the dog
Wechselstube bureau de change
Wegen Umbauarbeiten geschlossen closed for alterations
Wir müssen draußen bleiben dogs to be left outside
Ziehen pull
Zimmer frei vacancies
Zoll customs
Zuschlagpflichtig supplement payable
Zutritt für Unbefugte verboten no admittance to unauthorized persons
Zu vermieten to rent

SMOKING

Can I have a packet of . . . ?
Kann ich eine Packung . . . haben?
kan ish īnuh packoong . . . hahben

Have you got a light?
Haben Sie/hast du Feuer?
hahben zee/hast doo foyer

Do you mind if I smoke?
Stört es Sie/dich, wenn ich rauche?
shturt ess zee/dish ven ish rowkuh

Do you smoke?
Rauchen Sie/rauchst du?
rowken zee/rowkst doo

I've given up.
Ich habe es aufgegeben.
ish hahbuh ess owf-gegayben

Try one of these.
Probieren Sie eine von diesen hier.
probeeren zee īnuh fon deezen heer

Excuse me, it's no smoking here.
Entschuldigung, hier ist Nichtraucher.
entshooldigoong heer ist nisht-rowker

I quite enjoy the occasional cigar.
Ich rauche ganz gern mal eine Zigarre.
ish rowkuh gants gairn mal īnuh tsigarruh

Do you have any pipe tobacco?
Haben Sie Pfeifentabak?
hahben zee pfifen-tabak

Rauchen verboten.
rowken fairbohten
No smoking.

SPORT

Let's go to the swimming baths.
Wollen wir ins Schwimmbad gehen?
vollen veer inss shvimmbaht gayen

Isn't there an outdoor pool?
Gibt es hier kein Freibad?
geept ess heer kīn frībaht

Is there a sports centre here?
Gibt es hier ein Sportzentrum?
geept ess heer īn shport-tsentroom

I'm going jogging – coming too?
Ich gehe joggen – kommen Sie mit?
ish gayuh djoggen kommen zee mit

How about a game of tennis?
Wie wär's mit einer Runde Tennis?
vee vairss mit īner roonduh tennis

Your serve.
Sie haben Aufschlag.
zee hahben owfshlahk

Good shot!
(football) Prima Schuß!; (tennis) Guter Ball!
preema shooss, gOOter bal

I'd like to hire a sailboard.
Ich möchte gern ein Windsurfbrett mieten.
ish murshtuh gairn īn vintsurf-brett meeten

Can we go sailing?
Können wir Segeln gehen?
kurnen veer zaygeln gayen

There's a football match on television.
Es ist ein Fußballspiel im Fernsehen.
ess ist īn fOOss-bal-shpeel im fairnzayen

SUGGESTIONS

What do you suggest?
Was schlagen Sie vor?
vass shlahgen zee for

Let's go to the beach/cinema.
Gehen wir an den Strand/ins Kino.
gayen veer an dayn shtrant/inss keeno

Let's leave.
Laß uns gehen.
lass oonss gayen

How about an ice cream/a beer?
Wie wäre es mit einem Eis/Bier?
vee vayruh ess mit īnem īss/beer

Why don't we hire a car?
Warum mieten wir nicht einen Wagen?
varoom meeten veer nisht īnen vahgen

Why don't you talk to her?
Warum sprechen Sie nicht mit ihr?
varoom shpreshen zee nisht mit eer

Why don't you complain about it?
Warum beschweren Sie sich nicht?
varoom beshvairen zee zish nisht

You should tell the manager about it.
Sie sollten es dem Geschäftsführer sagen.
zee zolten ess daym geshefts-fewrer zahgen

How about it?, what do you say?
Wie wär's?, was sagen Sie dazu?
vee vayrss vass zahgen zee dahtsoo

SURPRISE

What a surprise!
Was für eine Überraschung!
vass fewr īnuh ewber-rashoong

Well, look who it is!
Sieh mal einer an, wer das ist!
zee mal īner an vair dass ist

Well well well!
Na ja!
na ya

Good heavens!
Ach du liebe Zeit!
ahK doo leebuh tsīt

Struth!
Heiliger Strohsack!
hīliger shtrohzack

That's amazing!
Das ist unglaublich!
dass ist oon-glowplish

That's terrible!
Das ist schrecklich!
dass ist shrecklish

I don't believe it!
Das gibt's doch wohl nicht!
dass geepts doK vohl nisht

How strange!
Wie merkwürdig!
vee mairkvewrdik

TALKING ABOUT ONESELF

My name is . . .
Ich heiße . . .
ish hīssuh

I am . . . years old.
Ich bin . . . Jahre alt.
ish bin . . . yahruh alt

I'm a teacher/doctor/taxi-driver.
Ich bin Lehrer/Arzt/Taxifahrer.
ish bin lairer/artst/taxifarer

I'm a hairdresser/nurse/teacher. (female)
Ich bin Friseuse/Krankenschwester/Lehrerin.
ish bin freezurzuh/kranken-shvester/lairerin

I come from . . .
Ich komme aus . . .
ish kommuh owss

I was born in London/Ireland.
Ich bin in London/Irland geboren.
ish bin in london/eerlant geboren

I was born in 1956.
Ich bin 1956 geboren.
ish bin noyn-tsayn-hoondert-zeks-oont-fewnftsik geboren

I live in . . .
Ich wohne in . . .
ish vohnuh in

I'm single/married/divorced.
Ich bin alleinstehend/verheiratet/geschieden.
ish bin alīnshtayent/fairhīrahtet/gesheeden

I have two children.
Ich habe zwei Kinder.
ish hahbuh tsvī kinder

TALKING TO PEOPLE

Do you speak English?
Sprechen Sie Englisch?
shpreshen zee eng-lish

What's your name?
Wie heißen Sie/heißt du?
vee hīssen zee/hīst doo

How old are you?
Wie alt sind Sie/bist du?
vee alt zint zee/bist doo

What do you do?
Was sind Sie/bist du von Beruf?
vass zint zee/bist doo fon berOOf

Where do you come from?
Woher kommen Sie/kommst du?
vohair kommen zee/kommst doo

Where do you live?
Wo wohnen Sie/wohnst du?
vo vohnen zee/vohnst doo

Are you married?
Sind Sie/bist du verheiratet?
zint zee/bist doo fairhīrahtet

Do you have any family?
Haben Sie/hast du Familie?
hahben zee/hast doo fameelee-uh

Have you ever been to Britain?
Waren Sie schon einmal in Großbritannien?
vahren zee shohn īnmal in grohss-britanee-en

TAXIS

Could you get me a taxi?
Könnten Sie mir ein Taxi besorgen?
kurnten zee meer īn taxi bezorgen

I'd like to book a taxi for tomorrow morning.
Ich möchte für morgen früh ein Taxi bestellen.
ish murshtuh fewr morgen frew īn taxi beshtellen

To the . . .
Zum/zur . . .
tsoom/tsOOr

How much is it going to cost?
Wieviel kostet das?
veefeel kostet dass

Could you stop here?
Könnten Sie hier anhalten?
kurnten zee heer anhalten

This is fine.
Hier ist gut.
heer ist gOOt

Can you wait for me/us please?
Können Sie bitte auf mich/uns warten?
kurnen zee bittuh owf mish/oonss varten

Can you take me/us back again?
Können Sie mich/uns wieder zurückfahren?
kurnen zee mish/oonss veeder tsOOrewk-faren

Can you come back at . . .?
Können Sie um . . . wiederkommen?
kurnen zee oom . . . veederkommen

TELEPHONING

Can I use your phone?
Kann ich Ihr Telefon benutzen?
kan ish eer telefohn benootsen

Hello, can I speak to . . . ?
Hallo, kann ich mit . . . sprechen?
halo kan ish mit . . . shpreshen

RESPONSES

(Einen) Moment.
(īnen) mohment
Just a minute.

Wer spricht bitte?
vair shprisht bittuh
Who's calling?

Am Apparat.
am aparaht
Speaking.

Er/sie ist nicht hier.
air/zee ist nisht heer
He/she's not here.

Can I leave a message?
Kann ich eine Nachricht hinterlassen?
kan ish īnuh nahKrisht hinterlassen

Please tell him/her that . . . called.
Bitte sagen Sie ihm/ihr, daß . . . angerufen hat.
bittuh zahgen zee eem/eer dass . . . an-gerOOfen hat

I'm at Hotel . . .
Ich bin im Hotel . . .
ish bin im hohtel

My phone number is . . .
Meine Telefonnummer ist . . .
mīnuh telefohn-noommer ist

Can you ask him/her to call me back?
Können Sie ihn/sie bitten, mich zurückzurufen?
kurnen zee een/zee bitten mish tsoorewk-tsooroofen

YOU'LL HEAR

Bitte warten.
bittuh varten
Please wait.

Kein Anschluß unter dieser Nummer.
kīn anshlooss oonter deezer noommer
Number unobtainable.

THANKS

Thank you.
Danke (schön).
dankuh (shurn)

> **Bitte (schön).**
> *bittuh (shurn)*
> You're welcome.

Thanks a lot, thank you very much.
Vielen Dank, vielen herzlichen Dank.
feelen dank feelen hairtslishen dank

That's very kind of you.
Das ist sehr freundlich von Ihnen.
dass ist zair froyntlish fon eenen

No thanks, no thank you.
Nein, danke.
nīn dankuh

Not for me thanks.
Für mich nicht, danke.
fewr mish nisht dankuh

Thank you for everything.
Vielen Dank für alles.
feelen dank fewr aless

Many thanks for your help.
Vielen Dank für Ihre Hilfe.
feelen dank fewr eeruh hilfuh

Could you thank him/her for me?
Könnten Sie ihm/ihr meinen Dank ausrichten?
kurnten zee eem/eer mīnen dank owss-rishten

He/she sends his/her thanks.
Er/sie läßt seinen/ihren Dank ausrichten.
air/zee lest zīnen/eeren dank owss-rishten

My ... has been stolen.
Mein/meine ... ist gestohlen worden.
mīn/mīnuh ... ist geshtohlen vorden

Our room has been broken into.
Jemand ist in unser Zimmer eingebrochen.
yaymant ist in oonzer tsimmer īn-gebroKen

Our car has been broken into.
Es ist in unseren Wagen eingebrochen worden.
ess ist in oonzeren vahgen īn-gebroKen vorden

Can you cancel my credit cards for me?
Können Sie meine Kreditkarten stornieren?
kurnen zee mīnuh kredeet-karten shtorneeren

All my money has gone.
Mein ganzes Geld ist weg.
mīn gantsess gelt ist vek

It was on the table/in the wardrobe/in my pocket.
Es war auf dem Tisch/im Schrank/in meiner Tasche.
ess var owf daym tish/im shrank/in mīner tashuh

I was only out for a couple of minutes.
Ich war nur für ein paar Minuten weg.
ish var nOOr fewr īn par minOOten vek

RESPONSES

Können Sie es beschreiben?
kurnen zee ess beshrīben
Can you describe it?

Waren Wertsachen dabei?
varen vairtzahKen dabī
Were there any valuables?

TICKETS

Two tickets for the pool please.
Zwei Karten für das Schwimmbad, bitte.
tsvī karten fewr dass shvimmbaht bittuh

Can I book two tickets for tomorrow night?
Kann ich zwei Karten für morgen abend reservieren?
*kan ish tsvī karten fewr morgen **ah**bent rezerveeren*

I'd like two singles to ...
Ich möchte gern zwei einfache Fahrkarten nach ...
*ish **mur**shtuh gairn tsvī īnfahKuh farkarten nahK*

I'd like a return to ...
Ich möchte gern eine Rückfahrkarte nach ...
*ish **mur**shtuh gairn īnuh rewkfarkartuh nahK*

RESPONSES

Wann fahren Sie zurück?
van faren zee tsOOrewk
When are you coming back?

Erste oder zweite Klasse?
*airstuh **oh**der tsvītuh klassuh*
First class or second?

For coming back the same day.
Zur Rückfahrt am selben Tag.
tsOOr rewkfart am zelben tahk

I'm/we're coming back in three days.
Ich komme/wir kommen in drei Tagen zurück.
*ish kommuh/veer kommen in drī **tah**gen tsOOrewk*

I'd like to change this ticket and go on Tuesday.
Ich möchte diese Fahrkarte umtauschen und am Dienstag reisen.
*ish **mur**shtuh deezuh farkartuh **oom**towshen oont am deenstahk rīzen*

TIME

(*see also DAYS*)

What's the time?
Wie spät ist es?
vee shpayt ist ess

Excuse me, can you tell me what time it is?
Entschuldigung, können Sie mir sagen, wie spät es ist?
entshooldigung kurnen zee meer zahgen vee shpayt ess ist

It's one o'clock.
Es ist ein Uhr.
ess ist īn OOr

It's ten past two.
Es ist zehn (Minuten) nach zwei.
ess ist tsayn (minOOten) nahK tsvī

It's a quarter past three.
Es ist Viertel nach drei.
ess ist feertel nahK drī

It's twenty-five past three.
Es ist fünf vor halb vier.
ess ist fewnf for halp feer

It's half past five.
Es ist halb sechs.
ess ist halp zeks

It's twenty to six.
Es ist zwanzig vor sechs.
ess ist tsvantsik for zeks

It's quarter to seven.
Es ist Viertel vor sieben.
ess ist feertel for zeeben

It's five to eight.
Es ist fünf vor acht.
ess ist fewnf for ahKt

It's just after nine.
Es ist kurz nach neun.
ess ist koorts nahK noyn

It's just coming up to ten o'clock.
Es ist kurz vor zehn.
ess ist koorts for tsayn

It's around three o'clock.
Es ist ungefähr drei Uhr.
ess ist oongefayr drī OOr

It's eleven o'clock exactly.
Es ist genau elf Uhr.
ess ist genow elf OOr

At eleven o'clock in the morning/at night.
Um elf Uhr morgens/abends.
elf OOr morgenss/ahbents

At what time?
Um wieviel Uhr?
oom veefeel OOr

It's getting very late.
Es ist sehr spät geworden.
ess ist zair shpayt gevorden

Early in the morning.
Frühmorgens.
frew-morgenss

In the early hours of the morning.
In den frühen Morgenstunden.
in dayn frewen morgen-shtoonden

Late at night.
Spät abends.
*shpayt **ah**bents*

Do we have time?
Haben wir Zeit?
***hah**ben veer tsīt*

There's plenty of time.
Wir haben reichlich Zeit.
*veer **hah**ben **rī**shlish tsīt*

Every two hours.
Alle zwei Stunden.
***a**luh tsvī **shtoon**den*

How long does it take?
Wie lange dauert es?
*vee **lang**-uh **dow**ert ess*

Half an hour.
Eine halbe Stunde.
***ī**nuh **hal**buh **shtoon**duh*

Five minutes.
Fünf Minuten.
*fewnf min**OO**ten*

Ages.
Ewig.
***ay**vik*

TOILETS

Can I use your toilet?
Kann ich Ihre/deine Toilette benutzen?
kan ish eeruh/dīnuh twalettuh benootsen

Where's the gents?
Wo ist die Herrentoilette?
vo ist dee hairen-twalettuh

Where are the ladies?
Wo ist die Damentoilette?
vo ist dee dahmen-twalettuh

I need to go for a pee.
Ich muß mal.
ish mooss mal

She's in the toilet.
Sie ist auf der Toilette.
zee ist owf dair twalettuh

Can I have some toilet paper?
Kann ich Toilettenpapier haben?
kan ish twaletten-papeer hahben

It won't flush.
Die Spülung funktioniert nicht.
dee shpewloong foonkts-yohneert nisht

Could you go and see if he's/she's all right?
Könnten Sie mal nachsehen, wie es ihm/ihr geht?
kurnten zee mal nahK-zayen vee ess eem/eer gayt

Abort, 00.
abort
Toilet.

Besetzt/frei.
bezetst/frī
Engaged/vacant.

Damen.
dahmen
Ladies.

Herren.
hairen
Gentlemen.

TRAINS

(*see also TICKETS*)

How much does the train to ... cost?
Wieviel kostet die Fahrt nach ...?
veefeel kostet dee fart nahK

Is this train going to ...?
Fährt dieser Zug nach ... ?
fayrt deezer tsOOk nahK

Which platform is it for ...?
Von welchem Gleis fährt der Zug nach ...?
fon velshem glīss fayrt dair tsOOk nahK

Is this the right platform for ...?
Ist dies das richtige Gleis nach ...?
ist deess dass rishtiguh glīss nahK

Do I have to change?
Muß ich umsteigen?
mooss ish oomshtīgen

Do we change here for ...?
Müssen wir hier nach ... umsteigen?
mewssen veer heer nahK ... oomshtīgen

What's this station called please?
Wie heißt dieser Bahnhof, bitte?
vee hīst deezer bahnhohf bittuh

When's the last train back to ...?
Wann fährt der letzte Zug zurück nach ...?
van fayrt dair letstuh tsOOk tsOOrewk nahK

Hauptbahnhof, Hbf.
howpt-bahnhohf
Central station.

UNDERSTANDING PEOPLE

Pardon?, Sorry?
Verzeihung?, Wie bitte?
fairtsī-oong vee bittuh

Could you say that very slowly?
Könnten Sie das ganz langsam sagen?
kurnten zee dass gants langzahm zahgen

Could you write that down?
Könnten Sie das aufschreiben?
kurnten zee dass owf-shrīben

I don't understand.
Ich verstehe nicht.
ish fairshtayuh nisht

What did he say?
Was hat er gesagt?
vass hat air gezahkt

Could you interpret for me?
Könnten Sie für mich dolmetschen?
kurnten zee fewr mish dolmetshen

Yes yes, I understand.
Ja, ja, ich verstehe.
ya ya ish fairshtayuh

Do you understand what I'm saying?
Verstehen Sie, was ich sage?
fairshtayen zee vass ish zahguh

Oh, I see!
Ach so!
ahK zo

WEATHER

What's the weather like?
Wie ist das Wetter?
vee ist dass vetter

It's a lovely day.
Es ist ein herrlicher Tag.
ess ist īn hairlisher tahk

What a horrible day!
Was für ein schrecklicher Tag!
vass fewr īn shrecklisher tahk

What's the forecast for tomorrow?
Wie ist die Wettervorhersage für morgen?
vee ist dee vetter-forhairzahguh fewr morgen

It's raining again.
Es regnet schon wieder.
ess raygnet shohn veeder

It's going to rain.
Es wird regnen.
ess veert raygnen

It'll clear up later.
Es wird später wieder aufklaren.
ess veert shpayter veeder owf-klaren

It's so incredibly hot.
Es ist ganz unglaublich heiß.
ess ist gants oonglowblish hīss

It's very cold.
Es ist sehr kalt.
ess ist zair kalt

WINTER SPORTS

Can I have a ski-pass?
Kann ich einen Skipaß haben?
kan ish īnen sheepas hahben

I'll meet you at the ski-tow.
Wir sehen uns am Skilift.
veer sayen oons am sheelift

I'm going to the beginner's slope.
Ich gehe zum Idiotenhügel.
ish gayuh tsoom idee-ohten-hewgel

I need to practise my turns.
Ich muß meine Wenden üben.
ish mooss mīnuh venden ewben

Let's try a slalom.
Wollen wir Slalom probieren?
vollen veer slahlom probeeren

How much is a toboggan?
Wieviel kostet ein Schlitten?
veefeel kostet īn shlitten

But you're an experienced skier.
Du bist aber ein geübter Skifahrer.
doo bist ahber īn ge-ewpter sheefarer

Is this slope safe?
Ist diese Piste sicher?
ist deezuh pistuh zisher

Careful, it's icy!
Vorsicht, es ist vereist!
forzisht ess ist fairīst

Lawinengefahr.
laveenengefar
Beware of avalanches.

Absturzgefahr.
ap-shtoortsgefar
Danger! Precipice!

WISHES

Wish you were here.
Ich wünschte, Sie wären/du wärst hier.
ish vewnshtuh zee vayren/dOO vayrst heer

I wish I could.
Ich wünschte, ich könnte.
ish vewnshtuh ish kurntuh

Best wishes. (as written on card)
Alles Gute.
aless gOOtuh

Give him/her my best wishes.
Ich wünsche ihm/ihr alles Gute.
ish vewnshuh eem/eer aless gOOtuh

He sends his best wishes.
Er läßt schön grüßen.
air lest shurn grewssen

Have a good journey.
Gute Reise!
gOOtuh rīzuh

Happy birthday!
Herzlichen Glückwunsch zum Geburtstag!
hairtslishen glewkvoonsh tsoom geboorts-tahk

Happy Christmas!
Frohe Weihnachten!
froh-uh vīnahKten

Happy New Year!
Frohes neues Jahr!
frohess noyess yar

And to you too.
Danke, gleichfalls.
dankuh glīshfalss

ENGLISH-GERMAN DICTIONARY

Cross-references in this dictionary are to the phrase and grammar sections in the preceding part of the book.

An asterisk against a verb indicates that this verb forms its past tense with **sein**. For more information on this see the section called PAST TENSE.

For an explanation of (+ *acc*) and (+*dat*) see the section on cases.

A

a ein, eine, ein; *see ARTICLES*
about (*approx*) ungefähr
above über (+*acc/dat*)
abroad im Ausland; **to go abroad** ins Ausland fahren
accelerator das Gaspedal
accent der Akzent
accept akzeptieren; *see ACCEPTING*
accident der Unfall; *see CAR ACCIDENTS*
accommodation die Unterkunft; *see ROOMS*
accompany begleiten
account (*bank*) das Konto
ache der Schmerz
adaptor (*for voltage*) der Adapter; (*plug*) der Mehrfachstecker
address die Adresse
address book das Adreßbuch
admission charge das Eintrittsgeld
adult der/die Erwachsene
advance: in advance im voraus
advertisement (*in paper*) die Anzeige; (*TV*) der Werbespot
advise raten (+*dat*)
aeroplane das Flugzeug
afraid: I'm afraid (of) ich habe Angst (vor+*dat*)
after nach
afternoon der Nachmittag; *see DAYS*
aftershave das Rasierwasser
afterwards danach
again nochmal
against gegen (+*acc*)
age das Alter
agency die Agentur
agent der Vertreter
aggressive aggressiv
ago: a week ago vor einer Woche
agree: I agree ich bin einverstanden; *see AGREEING*
AIDS Aids
air die Luft
air-conditioning die Klimaanlage
air hostess die Stewardeß
airline die Fluglinie
airmail: by airmail per Luftpost
airport der Flughafen; *see FLYING*
alarm der Alarm
alarm clock der Wecker
alcohol der Alkohol
alive lebendig
all: all Germans alle Deutschen; **all the milk/beer** alle Milch/alles Bier; **all day** den ganzen Tag; **that's all** das ist alles
allergic to allergisch gegen (+*acc*)
alleyway die Gasse
all-inclusive Inklusiv-
allow erlauben
allowed erlaubt
all right: that's all right okay
almost fast
alone allein
Alps die Alpen *pl*
already schon
also auch
alternator die Lichtmaschine
although obwohl

altogether insgesamt
always immer
a.m.: 7 a.m. 7 Uhr morgens
ambassador der Botschafter, die Botschafterin
ambulance der Krankenwagen
America Amerika
American amerikanisch; (*man*) der Amerikaner; (*woman*) die Amerikanerin
among unter (+*acc*)
amp: 13-amp mit 13 Ampere
ancestor der Vorfahr
anchor der Anker
ancient alt
and und
angina die Angina
angry böse
animal das Tier
ankle der Knöchel
anniversary (*wedding*) der Hochzeitstag
annoying ärgerlich
anorak der Anorak
another ein anderer, eine andere, ein anderes; **another beer** noch ein Bier
answer die Antwort; (*verb*) antworten
ant die Ameise
antibiotic das Antibiotikum
antifreeze das Frostschutzmittel
antihistamine das Antihistamin
antique: it's an antique es ist antik
antique shop der Antiquitätenladen
antiseptic das Antiseptikum
any: have you got any bread/eggs? haben Sie Brot/Eier?; **I don't have any** ich habe keins/keine
anybody jemand
anyway sowieso
apart from außer
apartment das Zimmer
aperitif der Aperitif
apologize sich entschuldigen
apology die Entschuldigung; *see APOLOGIES*
appalling entsetzlich
appendicitis die Blinddarmentzündung
appetite der Appetit
apple der Apfel
apple pie der Apfelkuchen
application form das Bewerbungsformular
appointment die Verabredung; (*with doctor*) der Termin
approve of: I don't approve of it ich bin damit nicht einverstanden
apricot die Aprikose
April der April
architect der Architekt, die Architektin
area die Gegend
arm der Arm
arrest festnehmen
arrival die Ankunft
arrive ankommen
art die Kunst
art gallery die Kunstgalerie
arthritis die Arthritis
artificial künstlich
artist der Künstler, die Künstlerin
as (*since*) da; **as fast as** so

schnell wie; *see* *COMPARISONS*
ashamed: to be ashamed sich schämen
ashtray der Aschenbecher
ask fragen
asleep: she's asleep sie schläft
asparagus der Spargel
aspirin das Kopfschmerzmittel
asthma das Asthma
astonishing erstaunlich
at: at the station am Bahnhof; **at Dagmar's** bei Dagmar; **at 5 o'clock** um 5 Uhr
Atlantic der Atlantik
atmosphere (*in group*) die Stimmung; (*weather*) die Atmosphäre
attractive attraktiv
audience das Publikum
August der August
aunt die Tante
Australia Australien
Australian australisch; (*man*) der Australier; (*woman*) die Australierin
Austria Österreich
Austrian österreichisch; (*man*) der Österreicher; (*woman*) die Österreicherin
automatic automatisch
autumn der Herbst
awake wach
awful furchtbar
axe das Beil
axle die Achse

B

baby das Baby
baby-sitter der Babysitter
bachelor der Junggeselle
back (*of body*) der Rücken; **to come back/go back** zurückkommen/zurückgehen; **at the back** hinten; **the back wheel/seat** das Hinterrad/der Rücksitz
backpack der Rucksack
bacon der Speck
bad schlecht
badly schlecht
bag die Tasche; (*suitcase*) der Koffer
bake backen
baker's die Bäckerei
balance das Gleichgewicht
balcony der Balkon
bald kahl
ball der Ball
ball-bearings das Kugellager
ball-point pen der Kugelschreiber
Baltic die Ostsee
banana die Banane
bandage der Verband
bank die Bank
bank manager der Geschäftsführer der Bank
bar die Bar
barbecue der Grill
barber der Friseur
barmaid die Bardame
barman der Barkeeper
basement das Souterrain
basket der Korb
bath das Bad
bathing cap die Badekappe
bathroom das Badezimmer

bath salts das Badesalz
bathtub die Badewanne
battery die Batterie
Bavaria Bayern
be sein*; *see PAST TENSE*
beach der Strand
beans die Bohnen
beard der Bart
bearing (*in car etc*) das Lager
beautiful schön
because weil
become werden*
bed das Bett; **single/double bed** das Einzelbett/das Doppelbett; **to go to bed** zu Bett gehen
bed and breakfast (*place*) die Pension
bed linen die Bettwäsche
bedroom das Schlafzimmer
bee die Biene
beef das Rindfleisch
beer das Bier
beer mug der Bierkrug
before vor (+*dat*); **before I go** bevor ich gehe
begin anfangen
beginner der Anfänger, die Anfängerin
beginning der Anfang
behalf: on behalf of the company im Namen der Firma
behaviour das Verhalten
behind hinter (+*acc/dat*)
beige beige
Belgian belgisch; (*man*) der Belgier; (*woman*) die Belgierin
Belgium Belgien
believe glauben
bell die Glocke; (*for door, at reception etc*) die Klingel
belong gehören (+*dat*)
below unter (+*acc/dat*)
belt der Gürtel
bend die Kurve
berth (*for yacht*) der Liegeplatz; (*in ship*) die Koje
beside neben (+*acc/dat*)
best: the best der/die/das beste
bet die Wette; (*verb*) wetten
better besser
between zwischen (+*acc/dat*)
beyond jenseits (+*gen*)
bicycle das Fahrrad
bidet das Bidet
big groß
bikini der Bikini
bill die Rechnung
binding (*ski*) die Bindung
bird der Vogel
biro (*tm*) der Kuli
birthday der Geburtstag; *see WISHES*
biscuit das Plätzchen
bit: a little bit ein bißchen
bite der Bissen; (*insect*) der Stich
bitter bitter
bitter lemon das Bitter Lemon
black schwarz
black and white schwarz-weiß
blackberry die Brombeere
bladder die Blase
blanket die Decke
bleach (*for toilets etc*) das Reinigungsmittel
bleed bluten
bless: bless you! Gesundheit!
blind blind
blinds das Rollo

blister die Blase
blocked blockiert
blond blond
blood das Blut
blood group die Blutgruppe
blouse die Bluse
blow-dry: to have a blow-dry sich fönen lassen
blown (*fuse*) durchgebrannt
blue blau
boarding pass die Bordkarte
boat das Schiff; (*smaller*) das Boot
body der Körper; (*car*) die Karosserie
boil kochen
bolt der Riegel; (*verb*) verriegeln
bomb die Bombe
bone der Knochen; (*in fish*) die Gräte
bonnet (*car*) die Motorhaube
book das Buch; (*verb*) buchen
bookshop die Buchhandlung
boot (*shoe*) der Stiefel; (*car*) der Kofferraum
border die Grenze
boring langweilig
born: I was born in 1970 ich bin 1970 geboren
borrow leihen
boss der Chef, die Chefin
both: both of them beide
bottle die Flasche
bottle-opener der Flaschenöffner
bottom der Boden; (*of body*) der Hintern; **at the bottom of the hill** am Fuß des Berges
bottom gear der erste Gang
bouncer der Rausschmeißer
bowl die Schüssel
bow tie die Fliege
box die Schachtel; (*larger*) der Karton
box office die Kasse
boy der Junge
boyfriend der Freund
bra der BH
bracelet das Armband
brake die Bremse; (*verb*) bremsen
brake drum die Bremstrommel
brake fluid die Bremsflüssigkeit
brake lining die Bremsbeläge *mpl*
brake shoes die Bremsbacken *fpl*
branch (*company*) die Zweigstelle; (*tree*) der Ast
brand (*of product*) die Marke
brandy der Weinbrand
brave mutig
bread das Brot; **white/wholemeal bread** das Weißbrot/das Vollkornbrot
break zerbrechen
break down (*car*) eine Panne haben
breakdown (*nervous*) der Nervenzusammenbruch
breakdown service der Abschleppdienst
breakdown vehicle das Abschleppfahrzeug
breakfast das Frühstück
breast die Brust
breastfeed stillen
breath der Atem
breathe atmen
breeze die Brise

brick der Backstein
bridge (*over river etc*) die Brücke
brief kurz
briefcase der Aktenkoffer
bright hell; (*day*) heiter
brilliant (*idea etc*) glänzend
bring mitbringen
Britain Großbritannien
British britisch
brochure die Broschüre
broke: I'm broke ich bin pleite
broken kaputt
broker der Makler
brooch die Brosche
broom der Besen
brother der Bruder
brother-in-law der Schwager
brown braun
bruise der blaue Fleck
Brunswick Braunschweig
brush die Bürste
Brussels sprouts der Rosenkohl
bucket der Eimer
budget (*for holiday etc*) der Etat
buffet meal das Büfett
building das Gebäude
bulb (*light*) die Glühbirne
bumper die Stoßstange
bungalow der Bungalow
bunk beds das Etagenbett
buoy die Boje
burn die Verbrennung; (*verb*) brennen
bus der Bus
business das Geschäft
business card die Visitenkarte
business trip die Geschäftsreise
bus station der Busbahnhof
bus stop die Bushaltestelle
busy (*person*) beschäftigt; (*streets*) belebt; (*telephone*) besetzt
but aber; **not . . . but . . .** nicht . . . sondern . . .
butcher's die Metzgerei
butter die Butter
butterfly der Schmetterling
button der Knopf
buy kaufen
by von (+*dat*); **by car** mit dem Auto

C

cabbage der Kohl
cabin (*ship*) die Kabine
cable das Kabel
cable car die Drahtseilbahn
café das Café
cagoule der Anorak
cake der Kuchen
cake shop die Konditorei
calculator der Taschenrechner
calendar der Kalender
call rufen; (*phone*) anrufen
calm down sich beruhigen
Calor gas (*tm*) das Butangas
camera die Kamera
campbed die Campingliege
camping das Camping
campsite der Campingplatz
camshaft die Nockenwelle
can die Dose; **I/she can** ich/sie kann; **can you . . .?** können Sie . . .?; *see PERMISSION, PRESENT TENSE*
Canada Kanada
Canadian kanadisch; (*man*)

der Kanadier; (*woman*) die Kanadierin
canal der Kanal
cancel streichen
candle die Kerze
canoe das Kanu
can opener der Dosenöffner
cap (*hat*) die Mütze
capital (*money*) das Kapital
capital (city) die Hauptstadt
captain der Kapitän
car das Auto
caravan der Wohnwagen
caravan site der Campingplatz
carburettor der Vergaser
card die Karte
cardboard die Pappe
cardigan die Wolljacke
car driver der Autofahrer, die Autofahrerin
care: to take care of aufpassen auf (+*acc*)
careful vorsichtig
car ferry die Autofähre
car hire die Autovermietung
car keys die Autoschlüssel *mpl*
car park der Parkplatz
carpet der Teppich
car rental die Autovermietung
carriage der Wagen
carrot die Mohrrübe
carry tragen
carry-cot die Säuglingstragetasche
car wash die Autowaschanlage
case (*suitcase*) der Koffer
cash: to pay cash bar zahlen
cash desk die Kasse
cash dispenser der Geldautomat
cassette die Kassette
cassette player der Kassettenrecorder
castle das Schloß
casual clothes die Freizeitkleidung
cat die Katze
catastrophe die Katastrophe
catch fangen; **which bus do I catch?** welchen Bus muß ich nehmen?
cathedral der Dom
Catholic katholisch
cauliflower der Blumenkohl
cause der Grund
cave die Höhle
ceiling die Decke
celebrate feiern
celebration die Feier
cemetery der Friedhof
centigrade Celsius; *see CONVERSIONS*
central heating die Zentralheizung
central station der Hauptbahnhof
centre das Zentrum
century das Jahrhundert
certificate die Bescheinigung
chain die Kette
chair der Stuhl
chairlift der Sessellift
chairman der Vorsitzende
chairperson der/die Vorsitzende
chalet das Chalet
chambermaid das Zimmermädchen
chance: by chance durch Zufall

change (*small*) das Kleingeld; (*verb*) wechseln; (*clothes*) sich umziehen; **to change trains** umsteigen*
changeable (*weather*) wechselhaft
Channel der Kanal
charge der Preis
charter flight der Charterflug
chassis das Fahrgestell
cheap billig
cheat betrügen
check prüfen
check-in die Abfertigung
cheers! prost!
cheese der Käse
chef der Koch, die Köchin
chemist's die Apotheke
cheque der Scheck
cheque book das Scheckheft
cheque card die Scheckkarte
cherry die Kirsche
chest die Brust
chestnut die Kastanie
chewing gum das Kaugummi
chicken das Huhn; (*food*) das Hähnchen
chickenpox die Windpocken
child das Kind
children's portion der Kinderteller
chilled (*wine*) gekühlt
chilly (*weather*) kühl
chin das Kinn
chips die Pommes frites *pl*
chocolate die Schokolade; **milk chocolate** die Vollmilchschokolade; **plain chocolate** die Bitterschokolade; **hot chocolate** der Kakao
choke (*on car*) der Choke
choose wählen
chop (*meat*) das Kotelett
Christian name der Vorname
Christmas Weihnachten; *see WISHES*
church die Kirche
cider der Cidre
cigar die Zigarre
cigarette die Zigarette
cigarette lighter das Feuerzeug; (*in car*) der Zigarettenanzünder
cinema das Kino
circle der Kreis; (*in cinema etc*) der Rang
citizen (*of country*) der Staatsbürger, die Staatsbürgerin
city die Stadt
city centre die Stadtmitte
claim form das Antragsformular
clarify klären
class die Klasse; **first class** die erste Klasse; **second class** die zweite Klasse
classical music die klassische Musik
clean (*adjective*) sauber; (*verb*) reinigen
cleansing cream die Reinigungscreme
clear klar
clever klug
client der Kunde, die Kundin
cliff die Klippe
climate das Klima

climber der Bergsteiger, die Bergsteigerin
climbing boots die Bergstiefel
clips (*on boot*) die Schnalle; (*on ski*) der Halteriemen
cloakroom (*coats*) die Garderobe
clock die Uhr
close (*verb*) schließen
closed geschlossen
cloth der Stoff
clothes die Kleider *pl*
clothes peg die Wäscheklammer
cloud die Wolke
cloudy bewölkt
club der Klub
clutch die Kupplung
coach der Bus; (*of train*) der Wagen
coast die Küste
coat der Mantel; (*jacket*) die Jacke
coathanger der Kleiderbügel
cockroach die Küchenschabe
cocktail der Cocktail
cocoa der Kakao
coconut die Kokosnuß
code (*dialling*) die Vorwahl; (*postal*) die Postleitzahl
coffee der Kaffee; **white coffee** der Kaffee mit Milch
coin die Münze
Coke (*tm*) die Cola
cold kalt; **I'm cold** mir ist kalt; (*illness*) die Erkältung; **I've got a cold** ich bin erkältet
cold cream die Feuchtigkeitscreme
collar der Kragen
colleague der Kollege, die Kollegin
collect (*person, laundry*) abholen
collection (*stamps etc*) die Sammlung
Cologne Köln
colour die Farbe
colour film der Farbfilm
comb der Kamm
come kommen*; **come in!** herein!
comfortable bequem
commercial kommerziell
Common Market die Europäische Gemeinschaft
compact disc die Compact-Disc
company die Firma
company car der Firmenwagen
compartment das Abteil
compass der Kompaß
compensation die Entschädigung
competitor der Konkurrent, die Konkurrentin
complain sich beschweren
complaint die Beschwerde
complicated kompliziert
compliment das Kompliment
component der Bestandteil
comprehensive insurance die Vollkaskoversicherung
compulsory obligatorisch
computer der Computer
concert das Konzert
concrete der Beton
condenser der Kondensator
condition (*proviso*) die Bedingung; (*state*) der Zustand

conditioner die Haarkur
condom das Kondom
conductor (*orchestra*) der Dirigent, die Dirigentin
conference die Konferenz
conference room der Konferenzsaal
confirm bestätigen
confusing verwirrend
congratulations! herzlichen Glückwunsch!
connecting rod die Pleuelstange
connection die Verbindung
constipated verstopft
consulate das Konsulat
contact (*get in touch with*) erreichen
contact lenses die Kontaktlinsen *fpl*
contacts (*of person*) die Beziehungen *fpl*
contraceptive das Verhütungsmittel
contract der Vertrag
cook der Koch, die Köchin; (*verb*) kochen
cooker der Herd
cooking utensils das Kochgeschirr
cool kühl
coolant das Kühlmittel
cooling system das Kühlsystem
cooperation die Zusammenarbeit
copy die Kopie
corkscrew der Korkenzieher
corner die Ecke
cornflakes die Corn-flakes
correct richtig
corridor der Flur
cosmetics die Kosmetika *npl*
cost die Kosten *pl*; (*verb*) kosten
cot das Kinderbett
cotton die Baumwolle
cotton wool die Watte
couchette der Liegewagen
cough der Husten; (*verb*) husten
country das Land
countryside die Landschaft; **in the countryside** auf dem Land
couple (*man and woman*) das Paar; **a couple of ...** einige ...
course: of course natürlich
cousin (*male*) der Vetter; (*female*) die Kusine
cow die Kuh
crab die Krabbe
crafts das Handwerk
cramp der Krampf
crankshaft die Kurbelwelle
crash der Zusammenstoß
cream (*food*) die Sahne; (*for skin etc*) die Creme
crèche die Kinderkrippe
credit card die Kreditkarte
credit note die Gutschrift
crew die Mannschaft
crisps die Chips *pl*
crockery das Geschirr
cross (*verb*) überqueren
crossing (*by sea*) die Überfahrt; (*pedestrian*) der Überweg
crossroads die Kreuzung
crowd die Menge
crowded voll
cruise die Kreuzfahrt
crutches die Krücken *fpl*
cry weinen

cuckoo clock die Kuckucksuhr
cucumber die Gurke
cup die Tasse
cupboard der Schrank
currency die Währung
current account das Girokonto
curry der Curry
curtain der Vorhang
custom der Brauch
customer der Kunde, die Kundin
customs der Zoll
cut schneiden
cutlery das Besteck
CV der Lebenslauf
cycling das Radfahren
cyclist der Radfahrer, die Radfahrerin
cylinder der Zylinder
cylinder head gasket die Zylinderkopfdichtung
Czechoslovakia die Tschechoslowakei

D

dad der Vati
damage beschädigen
damn! verdammt
damp feucht
dance tanzen; *see DANCING*
danger die Gefahr
dangerous gefährlich
Danish dänisch
dare wagen
dark dunkel
dashboard das Armaturenbrett
data processing die Datenverarbeitung
date (*appointment*) der Termin; (*time*) das Datum
daughter die Tochter
daughter-in-law die Schwiegertochter
day der Tag
dead tot
deaf taub
deal der Handel; **it's a deal** abgemacht
dealer der Händler
dear (*expensive*) teuer
death der Tod
debt die Schulden *fpl*
decaffeinated koffeinfrei
December der Dezember
decide entscheiden
decision die Entscheidung
deck das Deck
deck chair der Liegestuhl
deep tief
degree (*measurement*) der Grad
delay die Verzögerung
deliberately absichtlich
delicious köstlich
demand fordern
Denmark Dänemark
dent die Beule
dentist der Zahnarzt, die Zahnärztin
dentures das Gebiß
deodorant das Deodorant
department store das Kaufhaus
departure die Abfahrt
depend: it depends das kommt darauf an
deposit (*as security*) die Kaution; (*first payment*) die Anzahlung
depressed deprimiert
dessert der Nachtisch

develop entwickeln
device das Gerät
diabetic: I'm diabetic ich bin Diabetiker(in)
dialect der Dialekt
dialling code die Vorwahl
diamond der Diamant
diarrhoea der Durchfall
diary das Tagebuch
dictionary das Wörterbuch
die sterben*
diesel (*fuel*) der Diesel
diet die Diät
difference der Unterschied
different verschieden
difficult schwierig
difficulty die Schwierigkeit
dining car der Speisewagen
dining room das Eßzimmer; (*in hotel*) das Speisezimmer
dinner das Abendessen; **to have dinner** zu Abend essen
dipped headlights das Abblendlicht
dipstick der Ölmeßstab
direct direkt
direction die Richtung
director (*of company*) der Direktor, die Direktorin
directory enquiries die Auskunft
dirty schmutzig
disabled behindert
disappear verschwinden*
disappointed enttäuscht
disaster die Katastrophe
disc brake die Scheibenbremse
disco die Diskothek
discount der Rabatt
disease die Krankheit
disgusting widerlich
disinfectant das Desinfektionsmittel
disk (*computer*) die Diskette
distance die Entfernung; (*gap*) der Abstand
distributor der Verteiler
district (*in town*) das Viertel
disturb stören
dive tauchen
divorced geschieden
do tun; **what does he do?** was macht er beruflich?; **that'll do nicely** prima
docks der Hafen
doctor der Arzt, die Ärztin
document das Dokument
dog der Hund
doll die Puppe
door die Tür
dormitory der Schlafsaal
double doppelt
double bed das Doppelbett
double room das Doppelzimmer
down: down there dort unten
down payment die Anzahlung
downstairs unten
draught der Zug
dream der Traum
dress das Kleid; (*verb: someone*) anziehen; (*oneself*) sich anziehen
dressing gown der Bademantel
drink das Getränk; (*alcoholic*) der Drink; (*verb*) trinken
drinking water das Trinkwasser
drive fahren*
driver der Fahrer, die Fahrerin

drive shaft die Kardanwelle
driving licence der Führerschein
drop der Tropfen; (*verb*) fallenlassen
drug (*narcotic*) die Droge
drunk betrunken
drunken driving Trunkenheit am Steuer
dry trocken; (*verb*) trocknen
dry-cleaner die chemische Reinigung
duck die Ente
durex (*tm*) das Präservativ
during während (+*gen*)
dustbin die Mülltonne
Dutch holländisch
Dutchman der Holländer
Dutch woman die Holländerin
duty (*tax*) der Zoll
duty-free zollfrei
duty-free shop der Duty-free-Laden
dynamo der Dynamo

E

each jeder, jede, jedes; **how much are they each?** was kosten sie das Stück?
ear das Ohr
early früh; (*too early*) zu früh
earrings die Ohrringe *mpl*
earth die Erde
east der Osten; **east of** östlich von (+*dat*)
Easter Ostern
East German DDR-
East Germany die DDR
easy leicht
eat essen
economy (*of country*) die Wirtschaft
economy class die Touristenklasse
EEC die EG
egg das Ei; **boiled egg** das gekochte Ei; **hard-boiled egg** das hartgekochte Ei
egg cup der Eierbecher
either . . . or . . . entweder . . . oder . . .
elastic elastisch
Elastoplast (*tm*) das Hansaplast (*tm*)
elbow der Ellbogen
electric elektrisch
electric blanket die Heizdecke
electricity der Strom
else: something else etwas anderes
elsewhere woanders
embarrassing peinlich
embassy die Botschaft
emergency der Notfall
emergency exit der Notausgang
empty leer
end das Ende
engaged (*toilet, phone*) besetzt; (*to be married*) verlobt
engine der Motor; (*train*) die Lokomotive
England England
English englisch; **the English** die Engländer
Englishman der Engländer
Englishwoman die Engländerin
enlargement die Vergrößerung

enough genug; **that's enough** das reicht
enter eintreten* in (+*acc*)
entertainment die Unterhaltung
entrance der Eingang
envelope der Umschlag
epileptic: he's epileptic er ist Epileptiker
equipment die Ausrüstung
especially besonders
estimate (*of costs*) der Kostenvoranschlag
Eurocheque der Euroscheck
Eurocheque card die Euroscheckkarte
Europe Europa
European europäisch
even (*number*) gerade; **even here/if** selbst hier/wenn; **even slower** noch langsamer
evening der Abend; *see HELLO*
every jeder, jede, jedes; **every time** jedesmal; **every day** jeden Tag; **every twenty minutes** alle zwanzig Minuten
everyone jeder
everything alles
everywhere überall
exaggerate übertreiben
example das Beispiel; **for example** zum Beispiel
excellent ausgezeichnet
except außer
excess baggage das Übergewicht
exchange tauschen
exchange rate der Wechselkurs
exciting aufregend
excuse me Entschuldigung!
executive der/die leitende Angestellte
exhaust der Auspuff
exhaust fumes die Abgase *npl*
exhibition die Ausstellung
exit der Ausgang; (*motorway*) die Ausfahrt
expenditure die Ausgaben *fpl*
expenses die Spesen *pl*
expensive teuer
experience die Erfahrung
explain erklären
export exportieren
exposure (*photo*) das Bild
exposure meter der Belichtungsmesser
express (*mail*) per Expreß
extension lead die Verlängerungsschnur
eye das Auge
eyebrow die Augenbraue
eyeliner der Eyeliner
eye shadow der Lidschatten

F

face das Gesicht
factory die Fabrik
faint in Ohnmacht fallen*
fair (*funfair*) der Jahrmarkt; (*trade*) die Messe; (*adjective*) gerecht
fall fallen*
false falsch
family die Familie
famous berühmt
fan der Ventilator; (*supporter*) der Fan
fan belt der Keilriemen
far (away) weit
fare (*travel*) der Fahrpreis

farm der Bauernhof
farmer der Bauer
fashion die Mode
fashionable modisch
fast schnell
fat das Fett; (*adjective*) dick
father der Vater
father-in-law der Schwiegervater
fault der Fehler; **it's my/his fault** ich bin/er ist schuld
faulty fehlerhaft
favourite (*adjective*) Lieblings-
fax das Telefax
fear die Angst
February der Februar
fed up: I'm fed up (with) ich habe genug (von +*dat*)
fee die Gebühr
feel fühlen; **I feel well/ill** ich fühle mich gut/schlecht; **I feel like** ich habe Lust auf (+*acc*); *see FEEL*
feeling das Gefühl
felt-tip der Filzstift
feminist feministisch
fence der Zaun
ferry die Fähre
fever das Fieber
few: few tourists wenig Touristen; **a few** einige
fiancé(e) der/die Verlobte
field das Feld
fight der Kampf; (*verb*) kämpfen
fill füllen
fillet das Filet
filling (*tooth*) die Plombe
film der Film
filter der Filter
financial finanziell
find finden
fine die Geldstrafe; (*weather*) schön; **fine!** gut!
finger der Finger
fingernail der Fingernagel
finish beenden
Finland Finnland
Finnish finnisch
fire das Feuer
fire brigade die Feuerwehr
fire extinguisher der Feuerlöscher
fireworks das Feuerwerk
firm (*company*) die Firma
first erste; (*firstly*) zunächst
first aid die Erste Hilfe
first class erster Klasse
first floor der erste Stock
first name der Vorname
fish der Fisch
fishbone die Gräte
fishing das Angeln
fishmonger's das Fischgeschäft
fit (*healthy*) fit
fix (*a date*) verabreden; (*in position*) festmachen
fizzy mit Kohlensäure
flag die Fahne
flash der Blitz
flash cube der Blitzwürfel
flat die Wohnung; (*adjective*) flach; (*tyre*) platt; (*battery*) leer
flat rate die Pauschale
flavour der Geschmack
flea der Floh
flight der Flug
flirt flirten
floor der Boden; (*storey*) der Stock
floppy disk die Floppy Disk
florist's die Blumenhandlung
flour das Mehl

flower die Blume
flu die Grippe
fluent: fluent German fließend Deutsch
fly die Fliege; (*verb*) fliegen*
fog der Nebel
fog light die Nebelleuchte
folk music der Folk
follow folgen* (+*dat*)
food das Essen
food poisoning die Lebensmittelvergiftung
foot der Fuß; **on foot** zu Fuß
football der Fußball
for für (+*acc*)
forbidden verboten
forehead die Stirn
foreign ausländisch
foreigner der Ausländer, die Ausländerin
foreign exchange die Devisen *pl*
forest der Wald
forget vergessen
fork die Gabel; (*in road*) die Gabelung
form (*document*) das Formular
fortnight: a fortnight vierzehn Tage
fortunately zum Glück
forward (*mail*) nachsenden
foundation cream die Grundierungscreme
fountain der Brunnen
four-star (*petrol*) das Super
foyer das Foyer
fracture der Bruch
frame (*of picture*) der Rahmen
frames (*of glasses*) das Gestell
France Frankreich
free frei; (*of charge*) gratis
freezer die Gefriertruhe
freight die Fracht
French französisch; **French woman** die Französin
Frenchman der Franzose
frequent häufig
fresh frisch
Friday der Freitag
fridge der Kühlschrank
friend der Freund, die Freundin
friendly freundlich
from: from Cologne to Munich von Köln nach München
front (*part*) die Vorderseite; **in front of** vor (+*acc/dat*); **the front wheel/seat** das Vorderrad/der Vordersitz
frost der Frost
frozen food die Tiefkühlkost
fruit das Obst
fruit juice der Fruchtsaft
fry braten
frying pan die Bratpfanne
fuel der Treibstoff
fuel tank der Tank
full voll
full beam das Fernlicht
full board die Vollpension
fun: to have fun sich amüsieren; **have fun!** viel Spaß!
funeral die Beerdigung
funnel (*for pouring*) der Trichter
funny (*strange, amusing*) komisch
furious wütend
furniture die Möbel *pl*
further weiter
fuse die Sicherung

future die Zukunft

G

game (*to play*) das Spiel; (*meat*) das Wild
garage die Garage; (*repairs*) die Werkstatt; (*petrol*) die Tankstelle
garden der Garten
garlic der Knoblauch
gas das Gas
gasket die Dichtung
gas permeable lenses die luftdurchlässigen Kontaktlinsen *fpl*
gastritis die Gastritis
gay homosexuell
gear der Gang
gearbox das Getriebe
gear lever der Schaltknüppel
generous großzügig
gentleman der Herr
gents (*toilet*) die Herrentoilette
genuine echt
German deutsch; (*man/woman*) der/die Deutsche
Germany Deutschland
get bekommen; **can you tell me how to get to ...?** können Sie mir sagen, wie ich zum/zur ... komme?; **it's getting cold** es wird kalt; **to get back** (*return*) zurückkehren*; **to get in** (*car*) einsteigen*; **to get off** aussteigen*; **to get up** aufstehen*; **get out!** raus!
gift das Geschenk
gin der Gin
gin and tonic der Gin Tonic
girl das Mädchen
girlfriend die Freundin
give geben; **to give back** zurückgeben
glad froh
glass das Glas
glasses die Brille
glove compartment das Handschuhfach
gloves die Handschuhe *mpl*
glue der Leim
go gehen*; (*by vehicle*) fahren*; **to go in** hineingehen*; **to go out** hinausgehen*; **to go down** hinuntergehen*; **to go up** hinaufgehen*; **to go through** hindurchgehen*; **to go away** weggehen*; **go away!** verschwinden Sie!; **it's all gone** es ist nichts mehr da
goat die Ziege
God Gott
gold das Gold
golf das Golf
good gut
goodbye auf Wiedersehen
good-looking gutaussehend
goods die Waren *fpl*
goose die Gans
gorgeous toll
got: have you got ...? haben Sie ...?
government die Regierung
grammar die Grammatik
grandfather der Großvater
grandmother die Großmutter

grapefruit die Pampelmuse
grapes die Trauben *fpl*
grass das Gras
grateful dankbar
gravy die Soße
greasy fett
Greece Griechenland
Greek griechisch
green grün
green card die grüne Karte
greengrocer's der Gemüsehändler
grey grau
grilled gegrillt
grocer's die Lebensmittelhandlung
gross brutto
ground floor das Erdgeschoß
group die Gruppe
guarantee die Garantie
guest der Gast
guesthouse die Pension
guide der Reiseführer, die Reiseführerin
guidebook der Reiseführer
guilty schuldig
guitar die Gitarre
gun (*rifle*) das Gewehr; (*pistol*) die Pistole
gynaecologist der Gynäkologe, die Gynäkologin

H

habit die Gewohnheit
hail (*ice*) der Hagel
hair das Haar
hairbrush die Haarbürste
haircut der Haarschnitt
hairdresser der Friseur, die Friseuse
hair dryer der Fön (*tm*)
hair spray das Haarspray
half die Hälfte; **half a litre/day** einen halben Liter/Tag; **half an hour** eine halbe Stunde
half board die Halbpension
hall die Halle; (*in house*) die Diele
ham der Schinken
hamburger der Hamburger
hammer der Hammer
hand die Hand
handbag die Handtasche
handbrake die Handbremse
handkerchief das Taschentuch
handle der Griff
hand luggage das Handgepäck
handsome gutaussehend
hanger der Kleiderbügel
hangover der Kater
happen geschehen*
happy glücklich; *see WISHES*
harbour der Hafen
hard hart
hard lenses die harten Kontaktlinsen *fpl*
hardly kaum
hat der Hut
hatchback das Hecktürmodell
hate hassen
have haben; **I have to ...** ich muß ...; *see PAST TENSE*
hay fever der Heuschnupfen
he er
head der Kopf
headache das Kopfweh
headlights die

Scheinwerfer *mpl*
health die Gesundheit
healthy gesund
hear hören
hearing aid das Hörgerät
heart das Herz
heart attack der Herzinfarkt
heat die Wärme
heater das Heizgerät
heating die Heizung
heavy schwer
heel die Ferse; (*of shoe*) der Absatz
height (*of person*) die Größe; (*of mountain*) die Höhe
helicopter der Hubschrauber
hello guten Tag; *see ATTENTION, HELLO, TELEPHONING*
helmet (*for motorbike*) der Helm
help die Hilfe; (*verb*) helfen (+*dat*)
helpful hilfreich
her (*possessive*) ihr, ihre, ihr; *see POSSESSIVES*; (*object*) sie, ihr; *see PRONOUNS*
herbs die Kräuter *npl*
here hier; **come here!** kommen Sie her!; **here you are** (*offering*) bitte sehr
hers: it's hers es gehört ihr; *see POSSESSIVES*
hiccups der Schluckauf
hide verbergen
high hoch
highway code die Straßenverkehrsordnung
hill der Berg
hillwalking das Bergwandern
him ihn, ihm; *see PRONOUNS*
hip die Hüfte
hire: for hire zu vermieten
hire purchase der Ratenkauf
his sein, seine, sein; **it's his** es gehört ihm; *see POSSESSIVES*
history die Geschichte
hit schlagen; (*hit record*) der Hit
hitchhike trampen*
hitchhiker der Tramper, die Tramperin
hitchhiking das Trampen
hobby das Hobby
hold halten
hole das Loch
holiday der Urlaub; (*public*) der Feiertag; **the summer holidays** die Sommerferien *pl*
Holland Holland
home: at home zu Hause; **to go home** nach Hause gehen*
homemade hausgemacht
homesick: I'm homesick ich habe Heimweh
honest(ly) ehrlich
honey der Honig
honeymoon die Flitterwochen *pl*
hood (*of car*) das Verdeck; (*of coat etc*) die Kapuze
hoover (*tm*) der Staubsauger
hope hoffen; **I hope so** hoffentlich; **I hope not** hoffentlich nicht
horn (*of car*) die Hupe
horrible furchtbar
horse das Pferd
horse riding der Reitsport
hospital das Krankenhaus

hospitality die Gastfreundschaft
hot heiß; (*to taste*) scharf
hotel das Hotel
hot-water bottle die Wärmflasche
hour die Stunde
house das Haus
housewife die Hausfrau
house wine der Tafelwein
hovercraft das Luftkissenboot
how? wie?; **how are you?** wie geht es Ihnen?; **how are things?** wie geht's?; **how many?** wie viele?; **how much?** wieviel?
hub die Radnabe
hub cap die Radkappe
humour der Humor
hungry: I'm hungry ich habe Hunger
hurry sich beeilen; **hurry up!** beeilen Sie sich!
hurt verletzen; **it hurts** es tut weh
husband der Mann
hydraulic hydraulisch
hydraulics die Hydraulik

I

I ich
ice das Eis
ice-axe der Eispickel
ice cream das Eis
ice lolly das Eis am Stiel
idea die Idee
idiot der Idiot
if falls
ignition die Zündung
ignition key der Zündschlüssel
ignition lock das Zündschloß
ill krank
immediately sofort
import importieren
important wichtig
impossible unmöglich
improve verbessern
in in (+*acc/dat*); **in 1960** 1960; **in English** auf englisch; **is he in?** ist er da?
inch der Zoll; *see CONVERSIONS*
included inbegriffen
incredible unglaublich
independent unabhängig
indicator (*car*) der Blinker
indigestion die Magenverstimmung
industrial industriell
industry die Industrie
infectious ansteckend
information die Informationen *fpl*
information desk die Auskunft
injection die Spritze
injured verletzt
injury die Verletzung
inner tube der Schlauch
innocent unschuldig
insect das Insekt
insect bite der Insektenstich
insect repellent das Insektenschutzmittel
inside (*in building, box etc*) drinnen
insomnia die Schlaflosigkeit
instant coffee der Pulverkaffee
instructor der Lehrer, die Lehrerin

instrument das Instrument
insulating tape das Isolierband
insurance die Versicherung
insurance policy die Versicherungspolice
intelligence die Intelligenz
intelligent intelligent
interest das Interesse
interested: to be interested in sich interessieren für (+*acc*)
interesting interessant
international international
interpreter der Dolmetscher, die Dolmetscherin
intersection das Autobahnkreuz
introduce (*person*) vorstellen
invitation die Einladung
invite einladen; *see INVITING PEOPLE*
invoice die Rechnung
Ireland Irland
Irish irisch
Irishman der Ire
Irishwoman die Irin
iron (*metal*) das Eisen; (*for clothes*) das Bügeleisen; (*verb*) bügeln
ironmonger's die Eisenwarenhandlung
island die Insel
it es
Italian italienisch
Italy Italien
itch das Jucken

J

jack (*car*) der Wagenheber
jacket die Jacke
jam die Marmelade
January der Januar
jaw der Kiefer
jazz der Jazz
jealous eifersüchtig
jeans die Jeans
jellyfish die Qualle
jeweller's der Juwelier
jewellery der Schmuck
Jewish jüdisch
job die Arbeit
jogging das Jogging; **to go jogging** joggen gehen
joint (*to smoke*) der Joint
joke der Witz
journey die Reise; *see WISHES*
jug der Krug
juice der Saft
July der Juli
jump springen*
jumper der Pullover
jump leads das Starthilfekabel
junction die Kreuzung
June der Juni
just: just two nur zwei; **I've just arrived** ich bin gerade erst angekommen; **just around the corner** gleich um die Ecke

K

keep behalten
kerb die Bordsteinkante
kettle der Wasserkessel
key der Schlüssel
key ring der Schlüsselring
kidneys die Nieren *fpl*
kill töten

kilo das Kilo; *see CONVERSIONS*
kilometre der Kilometer; *see CONVERSIONS*
kind freundlich; (*type*) die Art
king der König
kiss der Kuß; (*verb*) küssen
kitchen die Küche
knee das Knie
knife das Messer
knit stricken
knock schlagen; (*on door*) klopfen
knock over umstoßen; (*car*) anfahren
know wissen; (*person, place*) kennen; **I don't know** ich weiß nicht; *see PRESENT TENSE*
knowledge die Kenntnisse *fpl*

L

label das Etikett
ladder die Leiter
ladies (*toilet*) die Damentoilette
lady die Dame
lager das helle Bier
lake der See
lamb das Lamm
lamp die Lampe
lamppost der Laternenpfahl
land das Land; (*verb*) landen*
landing (*in house*) der Treppenabsatz
landscape die Landschaft
lane (*alleyway*) die Gasse; (*on motorway*) die Spur; (*small road in country*) das Landsträßchen
language die Sprache
language school die Sprachenschule
large groß
last letzte; **last year** letztes Jahr; **at last** endlich
late spät; **to be/arrive late** zu spät kommen*/ankommen*
later später
laugh lachen
launderette der Waschsalon
laundry (*to wash*) die Wäsche; (*place*) die Wäscherei
law das Gesetz
lawn der Rasen
lawyer der Rechtsanwalt, die Rechtsanwältin
laxative das Abführmittel
lazy faul
lead (*road*) führen
lead-free bleifrei
leaf das Blatt
leaflet der Handzettel
leak das Leck
learn lernen
least: at least mindestens
leather das Leder
leave lassen; (*go away*) abreisen*; (*forget*) vergessen
left links; **on the left (of)** links (von+*dat*)
left-hand drive die Linkssteuerung
left-handed: to be left-handed Linkshänder(in) sein
left luggage die Gepäckaufbewahrung
leg das Bein
lemon die Zitrone

lemonade die Limonade
lemon tea der Zitronentee
lend leihen
length die Länge
lens die Linse
less weniger
lesson die Stunde
let (*allow*) lassen
letter der Brief
letterbox der Briefkasten
lettuce der Kopfsalat
level crossing der Bahnübergang
lever der Hebel
library die Bücherei
licence die Genehmigung; (*driving*) der Führerschein
lid der Deckel
lie (*say untruth*) lügen
lie down sich hinlegen
life das Leben
life belt der Rettungsgürtel
life buoy der Rettungsring
life guard der Rettungsschwimmer, die Rettungsschwimmerin
life jacket die Schwimmweste
lift (*elevator*) der Fahrstuhl; **to give a lift to** mitnehmen
lift pass der Liftpaß
light das Licht; **have you got a light?** haben Sie Feuer?; (*adjective*) leicht; **light blue** hellblau; (*verb*) anzünden
light bulb die Glühbirne
lighter das Feuerzeug
lighthouse der Leuchtturm
light meter der Belichtungsmesser
lightning der Blitz
like mögen; **I would like ...** ich möchte gern ...; (*as*) wie; *see LIKES*
lilo die Luftmatratze
lip die Lippe
lipstick der Lippenstift
liqueur der Likör
list die Liste
listen (to) zuhören (+*dat*)
litre der Liter; *see CONVERSIONS*
litter der Abfall
litterbin der Abfallkorb
little klein; **a little bit (of)** ein bißchen
live leben; (*in town etc*) wohnen
liver die Leber
living room das Wohnzimmer
load (*on lorry etc*) die Ladung
loan der Kredit
lobster der Hummer
lock das Schloß; (*verb*) abschließen
locker das Schließfach
lollipop der Lutscher
lonely einsam
long lang
long-distance call das Ferngespräch
long-term langfristig
loo die Toilette; (*slang word*) das Klo
look (*seem*) scheinen; **to look at** ansehen; **to look like** ähneln (+*dat*); **to look for** suchen; **look out!** Achtung!; **I looked everywhere** ich habe überall gesucht
loose (*nut, handle etc*) lose
lorry der Lastwagen
lose verlieren
lost property office das Fundbüro

lot: a lot (of) viel
loud laut
lounge der Salon
love die Liebe; (*verb*) lieben; **to make love to** schlafen mit (+*dat*)
lovely herrlich
low tief
luck das Glück; **good luck!** viel Glück!
luggage das Gepäck
lukewarm lauwarm
lunch das Mittagessen
lungs die Lunge
Luxembourg Luxemburg

M

macho macho
mad verrückt; (*angry*) sauer
magazine das Magazin
maiden name der Mädchenname
mail die Post
main Haupt-
main road die Hauptstraße
make machen; **made of silver** aus Silber; **we'll never make it** das schaffen wir nie
make-up das Make-up
male chauvinist pig der Chauvi
man der Mann
manager der Geschäftsführer
many viele
map die Landkarte; (*of town*) der Stadtplan
March der März
margarine die Margarine
market der Markt
marmalade die Orangenmarmelade
marriage die Ehe
married verheiratet
mascara die Wimperntusche
mass (*church*) der Gottesdienst
match (*light*) das Streichholz; (*sport*) das Spiel
material der Stoff
matter: it doesn't matter das macht nichts; **what's the matter?** was ist los?
mattress die Matratze
May der Mai
maybe vielleicht
mayonnaise die Mayonnaise
me mich, mir; **for me** für mich; **me too** ich auch; **it's me** ich bin's; *see PRONOUNS*
meal die Mahlzeit; **enjoy your meal!** guten Appetit!
mean bedeuten; (*person: with money*) geizig
measles die Masern *pl*; **German measles** die Röteln *pl*
measurements die Maße *npl*
meat das Fleisch
mechanic der Mechaniker
medicine die Medizin
Mediterranean das Mittelmeer
medium (*steak*) medium
medium-sized mittelgroß
meet treffen
meeting das Treffen; (*business*) die Besprechung
meeting place der Treffpunkt
melon die Melone

member das Mitglied
membership card die Mitgliedskarte
mend reparieren
menu die Speisekarte; **set menu** die Tageskarte
mess das Durcheinander
message die Nachricht
metal das Metall
metre der Meter; *see CONVERSIONS*
midday der Mittag
middle die Mitte
midnight die Mitternacht
mild (*taste, weather*) mild
mile die Meile; *see CONVERSIONS*
milk die Milch
milkshake der Milchshake
minced meat das Hackfleisch
mind: do you mind if I...? stört es Sie, wenn ich...?; **I don't mind** das ist mir egal
mine: it's mine es gehört mir; *see POSSESSIVES*
mineral water das Mineralwasser
minute die Minute
mirror der Spiegel
Miss Fräulein, Frl.
miss vermissen; (*train etc*) verpassen; **there's one missing** eins fehlt
mistake der Fehler
misunderstand mißverstehen
misunderstanding das Mißverständnis
mix mischen
mixture die Mischung
model das Modell
modern modern
moisturizer die Feuchtigkeitscreme
Monday der Montag
money das Geld
month der Monat
monument das Denkmal
mood die Stimmung
moon der Mond
moped das Moped
more mehr; **no more...** keine... mehr; *see COMPARISONS*
morning der Morgen; *see HELLO*
mosquito die Stechmücke
most (of) das meiste (von); **most people** die meisten Leute; *see COMPARISONS*
mother die Mutter
mother-in-law die Schwiegermutter
motorbike das Motorrad
motorist der Autofahrer, die Autofahrerin
motorway die Autobahn
mountain der Berg
mountaineering das Bergsteigen
mouse die Maus
moustache der Schnurrbart
mouth der Mund
move sich bewegen; (*get something out of way*) aus dem Weg räumen
Mr Herr
Mrs Frau
Ms Frau
much viel
multi-storey car park das Parkhaus
mum die Mutti
Munich München
muscle der Muskel

museum das Museum
mushrooms die Pilze *mpl*
music die Musik; (*written*) die Noten *fpl*
mussels die Muscheln *fpl*
must: I/you must ich muß/Sie müssen; **you must not** Sie dürfen nicht; *see NECESSITY, PRESENT TENSE*
mustard der Senf
my mein, meine, mein; *see POSSESSIVES*

N

nail (*finger, in wood*) der Nagel
nail clippers der Nagelzwicker
nailfile die Nagelfeile
nail varnish der Nagellack
nail varnish remover der Nagellackentferner
naked nackt
name der Name; *see TALKING TO PEOPLE*
napkin die Serviette
nappy die Windel
nappy-liners die Windeleinlagen *fpl*
narrow eng
national national
nationality die Staatsangehörigkeit
natural(ly) natürlich
nature die Natur
near nah(e) (+*dat*); **near here/there** in der Nähe; **the nearest ...** der/die/das nächste ...
nearly fast
neat (*drink*) pur; (*room, appearance*) ordentlich
necessary notwendig; *see NECESSITY*
neck der Hals
necklace die Halskette
need brauchen
needle die Nadel
negative (*film*) das Negativ
negotiate verhandeln
negotiations die Verhandlungen *fpl*
neighbour der Nachbar, die Nachbarin
neither ... nor ... weder ... noch
nephew der Neffe
nervous nervös
net das Netz; **£500 net** £500 netto
neurotic neurotisch
neutral (*gear*) der Leerlauf
never nie
new neu
news die Nachrichten *fpl*
newsagent der Zeitungshändler
newspaper die Zeitung
New Year das Neujahr; *see WISHES*
next nächste; **next year** nächstes Jahr; **next to** neben (+*dat*)
nice nett; (*food*) gut
nickname der Spitzname
niece die Nichte
night die Nacht; *see HELLO*
nightclub der Nachtklub
nightdress das Nachthemd
nightmare der Alptraum
no nein; **no ...** kein ...; *see NEGATIVES*
nobody niemand

noise der Lärm
noisy laut
non-alcoholic alkoholfrei
nonsense der Unsinn
non-smoking Nichtraucher
no-one niemand
normal normal
north der Norden; **north of** nördlich von (+*dat*)
Northern Ireland Nordirland
Norway Norwegen
Norwegian norwegisch
nose die Nase
nosey neugierig
not nicht; *see NEGATIVES*
note (*money*) der Geldschein
notebook das Notizbuch
nothing nichts
novel der Roman
November der November
now jetzt
nowhere nirgends
number die Nummer
number plate das Nummernschild
nurse die Krankenschwester; (*male*) der Krankenpfleger
nut (*to eat*) die Nuß; (*for bolt*) die Mutter

O

obnoxious widerwärtig
obvious offensichtlich
occasion die Gelegenheit
occasionally gelegentlich
octane rating die Oktanzahl
October der Oktober
odd (*number*) ungerade; (*strange*) merkwürdig
of von (+*dat*); **of this** hiervon; **of that** davon; *see CASES*
off (*lights*) aus
offer anbieten
office das Büro
official offiziell; (*noun*) der Beamte, die Beamtin
often oft
oil das Öl
oil change der Ölwechsel
oil filter der Ölfilter
oil pressure der Öldruck
ointment die Salbe
OK okay; **I'm OK** mir geht's gut
old alt; *see TALKING TO PEOPLE*
old-age pensioner der Rentner, die Rentnerin
old-fashioned altmodisch
old town die Altstadt
olive die Olive
omelette das Omelett
on auf (+*acc/dat*); (*lights*) an; *see DAYS*
once einmal
one ein, *f* eine; *see NUMBERS*
onion die Zwiebel
onion soup die Zwiebelsuppe
only nur
open (*adjective*) offen; (*verb*) öffnen
opening times die Öffnungszeiten
opera die Oper
operation die Operation
operator (*telephone*) die Vermittlung
opportunity die Gelegenheit

opposite das Gegenteil; **opposite the hotel** gegenüber dem Hotel
optician der Augenarzt, die Augenärztin
optimistic optimistisch
or oder
orange die Orange; (*colour*) orange
orange juice der Orangensaft
orchestra das Orchester
order (*command*) befehlen; (*commercially, meal*) bestellen; (*noun*) die Bestellung
organization (*company etc*) die Organisation
organize organisieren
original original
other andere
otherwise sonst
our unser, unsere, unser; *see POSSESSIVES*
ours: it's ours es gehört uns; *see POSSESSIVES*
out aus; **he's out** er ist nicht da; **we're out of petrol** wir haben kein Benzin mehr
outside außen
oven der Backofen
over (*above*) über; (*finished*) vorbei; **over there** dort drüben
overdone verkocht
overnight (*stay, travel*) über Nacht
overtake überholen
owe schulden
own (*verb*) besitzen; **my own car** mein eigenes Auto
owner der Besitzer, die Besitzerin
oyster die Auster

P

pack packen
package das Paket
package tour die Pauschalreise
packed lunch das Lunchpaket
packet (*of cigarettes etc*) die Schachtel
page die Seite; (*verb: person in hotel etc*) ausrufen lassen
pain der Schmerz
painful schmerzhaft
painkiller das Schmerzmittel
paint die Farbe; (*on car*) der Lack; (*verb*) streichen
paint brush (*artist's*) der Pinsel
painting das Gemälde
pair das Paar; **a pair of shoes** ein Paar Schuhe
palace der Palast
pancake der Pfannkuchen
panic die Panik
panties das Höschen
paper das Papier
papers (*passport, driving licence etc*) die Papiere *npl*
paraffin das Paraffinöl
parcel das Paket
pardon? bitte?
parents die Eltern *pl*
park der Park; (*verb*) parken
parking lights die Parkleuchten *fpl*
parking place der Parkplatz
partner (*personal, in business*) der Partner, die Partnerin

party (*celebration*) die Fete; (*group*) die Gruppe; (*political*) die Partei
pass (*mountain*) der Paß; (*verb:hand*) reichen; (*move past*) vorbeigehen* an (+*dat*); (*in car*) vorbeifahren* an (+*dat*)
passenger der Passagier
passport der Paß
pasta die Nudeln *fpl*
pâté die Pastete
path der Weg
patience die Geduld
patient (*adjective*) geduldig
pavement der Bürgersteig
pay zahlen
payment die Zahlung
payphone der Münzfernsprecher
peach der Pfirsich
peanuts die Erdnüsse *fpl*
pear die Birne
peas die Erbsen *fpl*
pedal das Pedal
pedestrian der Fußgänger, die Fußgängerin
pedestrian crossing der Fußgängerüberweg
pedestrian precinct die Fußgängerzone
pen der Stift
pencil der Bleistift
pencil sharpener der Spitzer
penicillin das Penizillin
penis der Penis
penknife das Taschenmesser
people die Leute *pl*
pepper (*spice*) der Pfeffer; (*vegetable*) die Paprikaschote
per: per day pro Tag; **per cent** Prozent
perfect perfekt
perfume das Parfüm
perhaps vielleicht
period die Periode
perm die Dauerwelle
permanent permanent
permit die Genehmigung
person die Person
personal persönlich
pessimistic pessimistisch
petrol das Benzin
petrol gauge die Benzinuhr
petrol pump (*at garage*) die Zapfsäule; (*in car*) die Benzinpumpe
petrol station die Tankstelle
petrol tank der Benzintank
phone (*verb*) anrufen
phone book das Telefonbuch
phone box die Telefonzelle
phone number die Telefonnummer
photocopy die Fotokopie
photograph das Foto; **to take a photograph of** fotografieren
photographer der Fotograf, die Fotografin
phrase book der Sprachführer
pickpocket der Taschendieb
pick up (*laundry, from airport etc*) abholen
picnic das Picknick
picture das Bild
pie (*fruit*) der Kuchen; (*meat*) die Pastete
piece das Stück
pig das Schwein
pigeon die Taube
piles die Hämorrhoiden *pl*
pile-up die Karambolage
pill die Pille

pillarbox der Briefkasten
pillow das Kopfkissen
pillowcase der Kopfkissenbezug
pilot der Pilot, die Pilotin
pilot light die Stichflamme
pin die Nadel
pineapple die Ananas
pink rosa
pins and needles das Kribbeln
pipe das Rohr; (*to smoke*) die Pfeife
piston der Kolben
piston ring der Kolbenring
pity: it's a pity das ist schade
pizza die Pizza
plain (*not patterned*) uni
plane das Flugzeug
plant die Pflanze
plastic das Plastik
plastic bag die Plastiktüte
plate der Teller
platform (*station*) der Bahnsteig
play (*theatre*) das Stück; (*verb*) spielen
pleasant angenehm
please bitte
pleased zufrieden; **pleased to meet you!** freut mich!
plenty: plenty of viel; **that's plenty** das reicht
pliers die Zange
plug (*electrical*) der Stecker; (*in sink*) der Stöpsel
plum die Pflaume
plumber der Klempner
p.m.: 4 p.m. 4 Uhr nachmittags, 16 Uhr; **10 p.m.** 10 Uhr abends, 22 Uhr
pneumonia die Lungenentzündung
pocket die Tasche
points (*in car*) die Kontakte *mpl*
poison das Gift
poisonous giftig
Poland Polen
police die Polizei
policeman der Polizist
police station die Polizeiwache
polite höflich
political politisch
politics die Politik
polluted verschmutzt
pond der Teich
pool das Schwimmbecken
poor arm; (*performance, quality*) schlecht
pop music die Popmusik
pop star der Popstar
popular beliebt
pork das Schweinefleisch
port (*drink*) der Portwein
porter (*hotel*) der Portier
Portugal Portugal
Portuguese portugiesisch
possibility die Möglichkeit
possible möglich; *see POSSIBILITIES*
post aufgeben
postcard die Postkarte
poster (*for room*) das Poster; (*in street*) das Plakat
poste restante postlagernd
postman der Briefträger
post office die Post
potato die Kartoffel
poultry das Geflügel
pound das Pfund; *see CONVERSIONS*
powder (*for face etc*) das Puder
power cut der Stromausfall
powerful stark

practical praktisch
practise üben
pram der Kinderwagen
prawn die Krabbe
prefer vorziehen
pregnant schwanger
prepare vorbereiten
prescription das Rezept
present (*gift*) das Geschenk; **at present** zur Zeit
president (*of country*) der Präsident, die Präsidentin
press (*newspapers*) die Presse
pretty hübsch; **pretty good** ganz gut
price der Preis
price list die Preisliste
priest der Geistliche
prince der Prinz
princess die Prinzessin
print der Druck; (*of photograph*) der Abzug
printed matter die Drucksache
prison das Gefängnis
private privat
probably wahrscheinlich
problem das Problem
procedure der Vorgang
produce produzieren
product das Produkt
profit der Gewinn
program(me) das Programm
prohibited verboten
promise das Versprechen; (*verb*) versprechen
pronounce aussprechen
pronunciation die Aussprache
propeller shaft die Antriebswelle
prostitute die Prostituierte
protect schützen
protection factor der Schutzfaktor
Protestant evangelisch
proud stolz
public öffentlich
publicity die Werbung
pudding (*dessert*) der Nachtisch
pull ziehen
pump die Pumpe
puncture die Reifenpanne
pure (*gold, silk etc*) rein
purple violett
purse das Portemonnaie
push schieben; (*button etc*) drücken; (*car*) anschieben
pushchair der Sportwagen
put tun; **where can I put my car?** wo kann ich mein Auto hinstellen?
pyjamas der Schlafanzug

Q

quality die Qualität
quarter das Viertel
quay der Kai
queen die Königin
question die Frage
queue die Schlange; (*verb*) Schlange stehen
quick(ly) schnell
quiet ruhig; **quiet!** Ruhe!
quilt das Federbett
quite ganz
quote (*from author*) das Zitat; (*price*) der Kostenvoranschlag

R

rabbit das Kaninchen
race (*biological*) die Rasse; (*sport*) das Rennen
radiator der Kühler; (*in room*) der Heizkörper
radio das Radio
rail: by rail per Bahn
railway die Eisenbahn
rain der Regen; (*verb*) regnen; **it's raining** es regnet
rainbow der Regenbogen
raincoat der Regenmantel
rape die Vergewaltigung
rare selten; (*steak*) englisch
rarely kaum
rash (*on skin*) der Ausschlag
raspberry die Himbeere
rat die Ratte
rate (*of exchange*) der Wechselkurs
rather ziemlich; **I'd rather** ... ich würde lieber ...
raw roh
razor der Rasierapparat
razor blade die Rasierklinge
read lesen
ready fertig
really wirklich
rear lights die Rücklichter *npl*
rearview mirror der Rückspiegel
rear wheels die Hinterräder *npl*
reason der Grund
reasonable (*price, person*) vernünftig
receipt die Quittung
receive erhalten
recently kürzlich
reception (*hotel*) die Rezeption
reception desk der Empfang
receptionist der Empfangschef, die Empfangsdame
recipe das Rezept
recognize erkennen
recommend empfehlen
record die Schallplatte; (*sport etc*) der Rekord
record player der Plattenspieler
red rot
red-headed rothaarig
red light district die Strichgegend
reduction die Ermäßigung
refrigerator der Kühlschrank
refund erstatten
registered mail das Einschreiben
registration number die Autonummer
regular regelmäßig
regulations die Bestimmungen *fpl*
relax sich ausruhen
reliable verläßlich
religion die Religion
remember sich erinnern an (+*acc*); **I remember** ich erinnere mich daran
rent die Miete; (*verb*) mieten; *see RENTALS*
repair reparieren
repeat wiederholen
reply die Antwort
report der Bericht
representative (*of company*) der Vertreter, die Vertreterin
reservation die

Reservierung
reserve reservieren
responsibility die Verantwortung
responsible verantwortlich
rest (*remainder*) der Rest; (*sleep*) die Ruhe; **to take a rest** sich ausruhen
restaurant das Restaurant
return ticket die Rückfahrkarte
rev counter der Tourenzähler
reverse (*gear*) der Rückwärtsgang
rheumatism das Rheuma
rib die Rippe
rice der Reis
rich reich; (*food*) schwer
ridiculous lächerlich
right rechts; **on the right (of)** rechts (von +*dat*); (*correct*) richtig; **right now** jetzt; *see AGREEING WITH PEOPLE*
right-hand drive die Rechtssteuerung
right of way die Vorfahrt
ring der Ring; (*on phone*) anrufen
ring road die Umgehungsstraße
ripe reif
river der Fluß
road die Straße
roadsign das Verkehrszeichen
roadworks die Straßenbauarbeiten *fpl*
rock der Felsen; (*music*) der Rock
rock climbing das Felsenklettern
roll (*bread*) das Brötchen
roof das Dach
roof rack der Dachgepäckträger
room das Zimmer
room service der Zimmerservice
rope das Seil
rose die Rose
rotten (*lousy*) mies
round (*circular*) rund; *see DRINKS*
roundabout der Kreisverkehr
route die Strecke
rowing boat das Ruderboot
rubber das Gummi; (*eraser*) der Radiergummi
rubber band das Gummiband
rubbish der Abfall; **rubbish!** Quatsch!; **these are rubbish** die sind nichts
rucksack der Rucksack
rude unhöflich
rug der Läufer
ruins die Ruinen *fpl*
rum der Rum
run laufen*; (*buses, trains etc*) fahren*
rush hour die Hauptverkehrszeit
rust der Rost

S

sad traurig
saddle der Sattel
safe sicher
safety pin die Sicherheitsnadel
sailboard das Windsurfbrett

sailing das Segeln
sailing boat das Segelboot
salad der Salat
salad dressing die Salatsoße
salary das Gehalt
sale der Verkauf; (*reduced price*) der Ausverkauf; **for sale** zu verkaufen
salesman der Vertreter
salmon der Lachs
salt das Salz
salty salzig
same: the same ... derselbe/dieselbe/dasselbe ...
sample das Muster
sand der Sand
sand dunes die Dünen *fpl*
sandwich das belegte Brot
sanitary towel die Damenbinde
Saturday der Samstag, der Sonnabend
sauce die Soße
saucepan der Kochtopf
saucer die Untertasse
sauna die Sauna
sausage die Wurst
savoury pikant
say sagen
scarf (*neck*) der Schal; (*head*) das Kopftuch
scenery die Landschaft
schedule: behind schedule verspätet; **the project's on schedule** das Projekt läuft nach Plan
school die Schule
science die Naturwissenschaft
scientist der Naturwissenschaftler, die Naturwissenschaftlerin
scissors die Schere
Scot der Schotte, die Schottin
Scotland Schottland
Scottish schottisch
scrambled eggs die Rühreier *npl*
scream schreien
screw die Schraube
screwdriver der Schraubenzieher
sea das Meer
seafood die Meeresfrüchte *pl*
seagull die Möwe
search suchen
seasick seekrank
seaside: at the seaside am Meer
season die Jahreszeit; **in the high season** in der Hauptsaison
seasoning das Gewürz
seat der Sitz; (*place*) der Platz
seat belt der Sicherheitsgurt
seaweed die Algen *fpl*
second zweite; (*in time*) die Sekunde
second class zweiter Klasse
second-hand gebraucht
secret geheim
security die Sicherheit
see sehen
seldom selten
selection (*of wines etc*) die Auswahl
self-service die Selbstbedienung
sell verkaufen
sellotape (*tm*) der Tesafilm (*tm*)
send senden
sender der Absender

sensible vernünftig
sensitive sensibel
separate(ly) getrennt
September der September
serious ernst
serve bedienen; (*tennis*) der Aufschlag
service der Service
service charge die Bedienung
service station die Tankstelle
serviette die Serviette
several mehrere
sew nähen
sex der Sex; (*gender*) das Geschlecht
sexist sexistisch
sexy sexy
shade der Schatten
shampoo das Shampoo
share teilen
shares (*financial*) die Aktien *fpl*
sharp (*knife, taste*) scharf
shave sich rasieren
shaving brush der Rasierpinsel
shaving foam die Rasierseife
she sie
sheep das Schaf
sheet das Laken
shell die Muschel
shellfish die Schaltiere *npl*
ship das Schiff
shirt das Hemd
shock der Schock
shock-absorber der Stoßdämpfer
shocking skandalös
shoe der Schuh
shoe laces die Schnürsenkel *mpl*
shoe polish die Schuhcreme
shoe repairer der Schuhmacher
shop das Geschäft
shopping das Einkaufen; **to go shopping** einkaufen gehen*
shopping bag die Einkaufstasche
shopping centre das Einkaufszentrum
shop window das Schaufenster
shore das Ufer
short kurz
short circuit der Kurzschluß
shortcut die Abkürzung
shorts die Shorts *pl*
shortsighted kurzsichtig
short-term kurzfristig
shoulder die Schulter
shout rufen
show zeigen
shower die Dusche; (*rain*) der Schauer
shut (*adjective*) zu; (*verb*) schließen
shutter (*photo*) der Verschluß
shutters (*window*) die Fensterläden *mpl*
shy scheu
sick: I feel sick mir ist schlecht; **I'm going to be sick** ich muß mich übergeben
side die Seite
sidelights das Standlicht
sign das Schild; (*verb: name*) unterschreiben
signature die Unterschrift
silence die Stille
silencer der Auspufftopf
silk die Seide

silver das Silber
silver foil die Alufolie
similar ähnlich
simple einfach
since (*time*) seit; **since I've been here** seit ich hier bin
sincere ehrlich
sing singen
single (*unmarried*) ledig
single room das Einzelzimmer
single ticket die Einzelfahrkarte
sink sinken*; (*in kitchen*) die Spüle
sister die Schwester
sister-in-law die Schwägerin
sit down sich setzen
site (*camping etc, place*) der Platz
situation die Situation
size die Größe
ski der Ski; (*verb*) skifahren*; *see WINTER SPORTS*
ski boots die Skistiefel *mpl*
skid schleudern*
skiing das Skifahren
ski instructor der Skilehrer, die Skilehrerin
ski-jump (*structure*) die Sprungschanze
ski-lift der Skilift
skin die Haut
skin cleanser der Hautreiniger
skinny dünn
ski-pants die Skihose
ski-pass der Skipaß
ski-pole der Skistock
skirt der Rock
ski run die Skipiste
ski slope die Skipiste
skull der Schädel
sky der Himmel
sleep schlafen
sleeper der Schlafwagen
sleeping bag der Schlafsack
sleeping pill die Schlaftablette
sleepy müde
slice die Scheibe
slide (*photo*) das Dia
slim schlank
slippers die Hausschuhe *mpl*
slippery glatt
slow(ly) langsam
small klein
small change das Wechselgeld
smell der Geruch; (*verb*) riechen
smile das Lächeln; (*verb*) lächeln
smoke der Rauch; (*verb*) rauchen; *see SMOKING*
smoking (*compartment*) Raucher
smooth (*texture, drink*) weich
snack der Imbiß
snail die Schnecke
snake die Schlange
sneeze niesen
snore schnarchen
snow der Schnee; (*verb*) schneien
snow chains die Schneeketten *fpl*
so so
soaking solution die Aufbewahrungslösung
soap die Seife
sober nüchtern
soccer der Fußball
society die Gesellschaft
sock die Socke
socket die Steckdose
sofa das Sofa

soft weich
soft drink das alkoholfreie Getränk
soft lenses die weichen Kontaktlinsen *fpl*
software die Software
sole (*of foot, shoe*) die Sohle
solution die Lösung
some: some beer etwas Bier; **some buttons** ein paar Knöpfe
somebody jemand
something etwas
sometimes manchmal
somewhere irgendwo
son der Sohn
song das Lied
son-in-law der Schwiegersohn
soon bald
sore: I've got a sore throat ich habe Halsschmerzen
sorry! Entschuldigung!; **I'm sorry** tut mir leid; *see APOLOGIES*
soup die Suppe
sour sauer
south der Süden; **south of** südlich von (+*dat*)
souvenir das Souvenir
spade der Spaten
Spain Spanien
Spanish spanisch
spanner der Schraubenschlüssel
spare parts die Ersatzteile *npl*
spare tyre der Ersatzreifen
spark plug die Zündkerze
speak sprechen; **do you speak ...?** sprechen Sie ...?
specialist der Spezialist, die Spezialistin
speciality die Spezialität
spectacle case das Brillenetui
spectacles die Brille
speed die Geschwindigkeit
speed limit die Geschwindigkeitsbeschränkung
speedometer der Tacho
spell buchstabieren; *see ALPHABET*
spend ausgeben
spice das Gewürz
spider die Spinne
spinach der Spinat
splendid prima
spoke die Speiche
sponge der Schwamm
spoon der Löffel
sport der Sport
spot (*on skin*) der Pickel
sprain: I've sprained my ankle ich habe mir den Fuß verstaucht
spring (*season*) der Frühling; (*in seat etc*) die Feder
square (*in town*) der Platz
stain der Fleck
stairs die Treppe
stamp die Briefmarke
stand stehen; *see DISLIKES*
star der Stern
start beginnen; **the car won't start** das Auto springt nicht an
starter (*car*) der Anlasser; (*food*) die Vorspeise
state (*condition*) der Zustand
statement (*bank*) der Kontoauszug
station der Bahnhof
stationer's der Schreibwarenladen

stay der Aufenthalt; (*remain*) bleiben*; (*in hotel etc*) wohnen
steak das Steak
steal stehlen
steep steil
steering die Lenkung
steering wheel das Lenkrad
stepfather der Stiefvater
stepmother die Stiefmutter
steward der Steward
stewardess die Stewardeß
sticky klebrig
still (*adverb*) noch; (*not moving*) still
sting stechen
Stock Exchange die Börse
stockings die Strümpfe *mpl*
stomach der Magen
stomach ache die Magenschmerzen *mpl*
stone der Stein
stop (*bus-*) die Haltestelle; (*verb*) anhalten; **stop!** halt!
store (*put in storage*) lagern; (*shop*) das Geschäft
storey das Geschoß
storm der Sturm
story die Geschichte
straight ahead geradeaus
strange (*odd*) seltsam
stranger der/die Fremde
strawberry die Erdbeere
stream der Bach
street die Straße
stress der Streß
strike der Streik
string die Kordel
stroke (*attack*) der Schlaganfall
strong stark
stuck: it's stuck es klemmt
student der Student, die Studentin
stupid dumm
suburbs die Vorstadt
success der Erfolg
successful erfolgreich
suddenly plötzlich
suede das Wildleder
sugar der Zucker
suggest vorschlagen; *see SUGGESTIONS*
suit der Anzug; **it suits you** es steht Ihnen
suitable passend
suitcase der Koffer
summer der Sommer
sump die Ölwanne
sun die Sonne
sunbathe sonnenbaden
sunblock die Sun-Block-Creme
sunburn der Sonnenbrand
Sunday der Sonntag
sunglasses die Sonnenbrille
sunny sonnig
sunrise der Sonnenaufgang
sunset der Sonnenuntergang
sunshine der Sonnenschein
sunstroke der Sonnenstich
suntan: you've got a good suntan du bist schön braun
suntan lotion die Sonnenmilch
suntan oil das Sonnenöl
supermarket der Supermarkt
supper das Abendbrot
supplement der Zuschlag
supply liefern
support (*load, weight*) tragen
sure sicher
surname der Nachname
surprise die Überraschung
surprising überraschend

suspension (*of car*) die Aufhängung
swallow (*by accident*) verschlucken
sweat schwitzen
sweater der Pullover
Sweden Schweden
Swedish schwedisch
sweet das Bonbon; (*to taste*) süß
swim schwimmen*
swimming das Schwimmen; **to go swimming** schwimmen gehen*
swimming costume der Badeanzug
swimming pool das Schwimmbad
swimming trunks die Badehose
Swiss Schweizer
switch der Schalter
switch off ausschalten
switch on anschalten
Switzerland die Schweiz
swollen geschwollen
synagogue die Synagoge
synthetic synthetisch

T

table der Tisch; (*of figures*) die Tabelle
tablecloth die Tischdecke
tablet die Tablette
table tennis das Tischtennis
tail der Schwanz
tailback der Rückstau
take nehmen; **to take away** (*remove*) wegnehmen; (*food*) zum Mitnehmen; **to take off** (*plane*) abheben; (*clothes*) ausziehen
talc das Körperpuder
talk sprechen; (*lecture etc*) der Vortrag
tall groß
tampon das Tampon
tank der Tank
tap der Wasserhahn
tape (*cassette*) die Kassette; (*sticky*) das Klebeband
tape recorder das Tonbandgerät
target (*objective*) das Ziel
tart die Torte
taste der Geschmack; (*verb: try*) probieren
tax die Steuer
taxi das Taxi; *see TAXIS*
taxi driver der Taxifahrer, die Taxifahrerin
taxi rank der Taxistand
tea der Tee
tea bag der Teebeutel
teach: will you teach me some German? können Sie mir etwas Deutsch beibringen?
teacher der Lehrer, die Lehrerin
team die Mannschaft
teapot die Teekanne
tea towel das Geschirrtuch
technical technisch
teenager der Teenager
telegram das Telegramm
telephone das Telefon
telephone box die Telefonzelle
telephone directory das Telefonbuch
television das Fernsehen; **on television** im Fernsehen; **to watch television** fernsehen

telex das Fernschreiben
temperature die Temperatur; (*medical*) das Fieber
temporary vorübergehend
tennis das Tennis
tent das Zelt
tent peg der Hering
terrible furchtbar
terrific sagenhaft
test ausprobieren
than als; *see COMPARISONS*
thank danken (+*dat*); **thank you** danke; *see THANKS*
that (*adjective*) dieser, diese, dieses; (*pronoun*) das; **I think that ...** ich glaube, daß ...; **that one** der/die/das da; *see REFERRING TO THINGS*
the der, die, das; *pl* die; *see ARTICLES*
theatre das Theater
their ihr, ihre, ihr; *see POSSESSIVES*
theirs: it's theirs es gehört ihnen; *see POSSESSIVES*
them sie, ihnen; *see PRONOUNS*
then dann
there da; **there is/are** es gibt; **is/are there ...?** gibt es ...?
thermometer das Thermometer
thermos flask die Thermosflasche
thermostat das Thermostat
these diese; *see REFERRING TO THINGS*
they sie
thick dick
thief der Dieb, die Diebin
thigh der Schenkel
thin dünn
thing das Ding
think denken
third party (*insurance*) die Haftpflichtversicherung
thirsty: I'm thirsty ich habe Durst
this (*adjective*) dieser, diese, dieses; (*pronoun*) dies, das; **this one** dieser, diese, dieses; *see REFERRING TO THINGS*
those (*adjective*) die; (*pronoun*) die da; *see REFERRING TO THINGS*
thread der Faden
throat die Kehle
throat lozenges die Halstabletten *fpl*
through durch (+*acc*)
throw werfen; **to throw away** wegwerfen
thumb der Daumen
thunder der Donner
thunderstorm das Gewitter
Thursday der Donnerstag
ticket die Karte; (*for travel*) die Fahrkarte; (*for plane*) das Flugticket
ticket office die Kasse; (*trains etc*) der Fahrkartenschalter
tide: high tide die Flut; **low tide** die Ebbe
tie die Krawatte
tight eng
tights die Strumpfhose
time die Zeit; **two/three times** zweimal/dreimal;

on time rechtzeitig; **what time is it?** wie spät ist es?; **next time** nächstes Mal; *see TIME*
timetable der Fahrplan
tin opener der Dosenöffner
tip das Trinkgeld
tired müde
tiring anstrengend
tissues die Papiertücher *npl*
to: to Berlin nach Berlin; **to the bank** zur Bank
toast der Toast
tobacco der Tabak
today heute
toe die Zehe
together zusammen
toilet die Toilette
toilet paper das Toilettenpapier
tomato die Tomate
tomorrow morgen; *see DAYS*
tongue die Zunge
tonight heute abend
tonsillitis die Mandelentzündung
tonsils die Mandeln *fpl*
too (*also*) auch; **too fast** zu schnell; **not too much** nicht zu viel
tool das Werkzeug
tooth der Zahn
toothache die Zahnschmerzen *mpl*
toothbrush die Zahnbürste
toothpaste die Zahnpasta
top: at the top oben
torch die Taschenlampe
touch berühren
tough (*meat*) zäh; **tough luck** Pech
tour die Rundreise; (*of castle etc*) der Rundgang
tourist der Tourist, die Touristin
tow abschleppen
towel das Handtuch
tower der Turm
tow line das Abschleppseil
town die Stadt
town hall das Rathaus
toy das Spielzeug
tracksuit der Trainingsanzug
trade union die Gewerkschaft
tradition die Tradition
traditional traditionell
traffic der Verkehr
traffic jam der Stau
traffic lights die Ampel
traffic warden die Politesse (*all female in Germany*)
trailer (*behind car*) der Anhänger
train der Zug
trainers die Turnschuhe *mpl*
tram die Straßenbahn; *see BUSES AND TRAMS*
transformer der Transformator
transistor (*radio*) das Transistorradio
transit visa das Transitvisum
translate übersetzen
translation die Übersetzung
translator der Übersetzer, die Übersetzerin
travel reisen*
travel agent's das Reisebüro
traveller's cheque der Reisescheck
tray das Tablett
tree der Baum
tremendous fantastisch
trip der Ausflug

trolley der Kofferkuli
trouble der Ärger
trousers die Hose
true wahr
truth die Wahrheit
try versuchen; **to try on** anprobieren
T-shirt das T-Shirt
tube (*tyre*) der Schlauch
Tuesday der Dienstag
tuna fish der Thunfisch
tunnel der Tunnel
Turkey die Türkei
Turkish türkisch
turn drehen; **to turn off** (*driving*) abbiegen*
tweezers die Pinzette
twice zweimal
twin beds die zwei Einzelbetten *npl*
twins die Zwillinge *mpl*
two-star (*petrol*) das Normalbenzin
typewriter die Schreibmaschine
typical typisch
tyre der Reifen
tyre lever das Montiereisen
tyre pressure der Reifendruck

U

ugly häßlich
umbrella der Regenschirm
uncle der Onkel
under unter (+*acc/dat*)
underdone nicht gar
underground die U-Bahn
underneath unten; **underneath ...** unter ... (+*acc/dat*)
underpants die Unterhose
understand verstehen; *see UNDERSTANDING PEOPLE*
underwear die Unterwäsche
unemployed arbeitslos
unfortunately leider
United States die Vereinigten Staaten
university die Universität
unleaded bleifrei
unpack auspacken
unpleasant unangenehm
until bis
unusual ungewöhnlich
up: up there dort oben
upside down verkehrt herum
upstairs oben
urgent dringend
us uns
use gebrauchen
useful nützlich
usual üblich
usually gewöhnlich

V

vacancy: they've got a vacancy (*room*) sie haben ein Zimmer frei
vacation die Ferien *pl*
vaccination die Impfung
vacuum cleaner der Staubsauger
vagina die Vagina
valid gültig
valley das Tal
valuable wertvoll
valve das Ventil
van der Kleinbus
vanilla die Vanille

vase die Vase
VAT die Mehrwertsteuer, MWSt.
VD die Geschlechtskrankheit
veal das Kalbfleisch
vegetables das Gemüse
vegetarian vegetarisch
vehicle das Fahrzeug
very sehr
vest das Unterhemd
vet der Tierarzt, die Tierärztin
via über
video das Video
video recorder der Videorecorder
Vienna Wien
view die Aussicht
viewfinder der Sucher
village das Dorf
vinegar der Essig
vineyard der Weinberg
visa das Visum
visit der Besuch; (*verb*) besuchen
vitamins die Vitamine *npl*
voice die Stimme
voltage die Spannung

W

waist die Taille
wait warten; **wait for me!** warten Sie auf mich!
waiter der Kellner; *see RESTAURANTS*
waiting room der Wartesaal
waitress die Kellnerin; *see RESTAURANTS*
wake up (*someone*) wecken; (*oneself*) aufwachen*
Wales Wales
walk der Spaziergang; (*verb*) zu Fuß gehen*; **to go for a walk** spazierengehen*
walking boots die Wanderstiefel *mpl*
walkman (*tm*) der Walkman (*tm*)
wall die Mauer; (*inside*) die Wand
wallet die Brieftasche
want wollen; **I want . . .** ich will . . .; **he wants . . .** er will . . .; **do you want . . .?** wollen Sie . . .? *see PRESENT TENSE*
war der Krieg
warden (*hostel*) der Herbergsvater, die Herbergsmutter
warehouse das Lager
warm warm
warn warnen
warning die Warnung
warning triangle das Warndreieck
wash waschen; (*oneself*) sich waschen
washbasin das Waschbecken
washer (*for bolt etc*) der Dichtungsring
washing die Wäsche
washing machine die Waschmaschine
washing powder das Waschpulver
washing-up der Abwasch
washing-up liquid das Spülmittel
wasp die Wespe
watch (*for time*) die Armbanduhr; (*take care of*) aufpassen auf (+*acc*)

water das Wasser
waterfall der Wasserfall
waterproof wasserfest
waterskiing das Wasserskilaufen
wave (*in sea, hair*) die Welle
way: this way (*like this*) so; **can you tell me the way to the ...?** können Sie mir sagen, wie ich zum/zur ... komme?; *see DIRECTIONS*
we wir
weak schwach
weather das Wetter; *see WEATHER*
weather forecast der Wetterbericht
wedding die Hochzeit
Wednesday der Mittwoch
week die Woche
weekend das Wochenende
weight das Gewicht
welcome! willkommen!; **you're welcome** bitte sehr
well: he's well/not well es geht ihm gut/schlecht; **to do something well** etwas gut machen; *see SURPRISE*
well done (*meat*) durchgebraten
wellingtons die Gummistiefel *mpl*
Welsh walisisch
Welshman der Waliser
Welshwoman die Waliserin
west der Westen; **west of** westlich von (+*dat*)
West German BRD-
West Germany die Bundesrepublik Deutschland
wet naß
what? was?; **what car?** welches Auto?
wheel das Rad
wheelchair der Rollstuhl
when? wann?; **when I got here** als ich hier ankam
where? wo?
which? welcher?, welche?, welches?
while während
whipped cream die Schlagsahne
whisky der Whisky
whisper flüstern
white weiß
Whitsun Pfingsten
who? wer?; **the man who ...** der Mann, der ...; **the woman who ...** die Frau, die ...
whole ganze
whooping cough der Keuchhusten
whose: whose is this? wem gehört das?
why? warum?
wide breit
wide-angle lens das Weitwinkelobjektiv
widow die Witwe
widower der Witwer
wife die Frau
wild wild
will *see FUTURE*
win gewinnen
wind der Wind
window das Fenster
window seat der Fensterplatz
window shopping der Schaufensterbummel
windscreen die Windschutzscheibe
windscreen washer die

Scheibenreinigungsanlage
windscreen wiper der Scheibenwischer
windsurfing das Windsurfen
windy windig
wine der Wein; **red/white/rosé wine** der Rotwein/Weißwein/Rosé
wine list die Weinkarte
wing der Flügel; (*car*) der Kotflügel
wing mirror der Seitenspiegel
winter der Winter
winter sports der Wintersport
wire der Draht
wiring diagram der Schaltplan
wish: best wishes alles Gute; *see WISHES*
with mit (+*dat*)
without ohne (+*acc*)
witness der Zeuge, die Zeugin; *see CAR ACCIDENTS*
woman die Frau
wonderful wunderbar
wood das Holz
woods der Wald
wool die Wolle
word das Wort
work die Arbeit; (*verb*) arbeiten; **it's not working** es funktioniert nicht
works (*factory etc*) das Werk
world die Welt
worry die Sorge; **don't worry** machen Sie sich keine Sorgen
worse schlechter
worst: the worst der/die/das schlechteste
wrap einpacken
wrapping paper das Packpapier
wrench der Schraubenschlüssel
wrist das Handgelenk
write schreiben
write-off (*car*) der Totalschaden
writing paper das Schreibpapier
wrong falsch; **he's wrong** er hat unrecht

X

X-ray die Röntgenaufnahme

Y

yacht die Jacht
year das Jahr
yellow gelb
yellow pages das Branchenverzeichnis
yes ja; **oh yes I do!** (*contradicting*) doch!
yesterday gestern; *see DAYS*
yet: not yet noch nicht
yoghurt der Joghurt
you Sie; (*familiar*) du; **for you** für Sie/dich; **with you** mit Ihnen/dir; *see PRONOUNS*
young jung
your Ihr, Ihre, Ihr; (*familiar*) dein, deine, dein; *see POSSESSIVES*

yours: it's yours es gehört Ihnen; (*familiar*) es gehört dir; *see POSSESSIVES*
youth hostel die Jugendherberge

Z

zero null
zip der Reißverschluß
zoo der Zoo
zoom lens das Zoomobjektiv